The Precious Moments Story

The Precious Moments Story

The Life And Work Of Samuel J. Butcher

Text by
Dallie Miessner

—

Photography by
Walter Pfeiffer

—

Published by
Portfolio Press,
Huntington,
New York

Contents

"God is not bound by time. Only we are. We should use it wisely to produce within our lifetime the things that will benefit the world when we are gone."

A panorama of pinks and golds slides across the eastern horizon as Sam Butcher leaves his studio and walks the short distance to his home where he will sleep until his work day begins a few hours later. Experience has proved he can be the most productive while his family and business associates sleep. But it is daytime in the Philippines and often at night he talks by phone with the manager of his factory in Iloilo City.

The originality and warmth of Sam Butcher's artwork has earned him a reputation as one of America's most prolific and gifted artists. The acceptance of his art has been rewarding, but he constantly strives for greater excellence. Always with him is paper on which he sketches what later become Precious Moments paintings. A man of deep insight and introspection, Sam feels he must use his talent, as well as the gifts God has given to him, wisely. Much of Sam's day is spent ministering to others.

Mid-morning finds Sam back in the studio, answering mail and calls. Then it's off for coffee with a family member or business associate. Much of Sam's day is spent behind the wheel of a car, for driving helps him relax while he works. In order to escape the constant interruptions in his studio, he often works in an area restaurant. He sketches, writes poetry, or discusses business with his assistant. The restaurant is his office away from the studio. By mid-afternoon Sam is ready for a nap, and often after fifteen minutes he is wide awake and returns to the studio to work again, sometimes until dawn.

Sam's wife Katie has also found a wellspring of creativity on their hilltop in southwest Missouri. Often sunrise finds her in the woods with her camera catching the last drops of dew on the petals of a wildflower. She may unexpectedly rush out of the house with her camera, to jump into the car and chase a rainbow. She is happy here and finds joy in baking bread and picking wildflowers. In addition to her music, writing and Bible study, her greatest joy has always been ministering to others.

The Butcher children, too, have the freedom to pursue their own interests, which include writing, painting and sculpting. Often the wild sweet strains of an original musical composition adds its own magic to the hillside.

From the second-story balcony off Kate's studio to the south, she can see the guest house down by the creek, or the chapel rising proudly on a nearby hillside. Off to the right she can see Debbie playing with her animals outside her log cabin home. Below the hill, in a little brown house, two of her sons are playing an original classical rock composition. In the house, Heather can be heard talking on the phone. Sam drives up and as he gets out of the car with a cup of coffee in his hand, he calls to Donny to join him, then heads for his studio.

At Home With Sam Butcher

Although Sam Butcher is known mainly for his Precious Moments art, he enjoys many other styles. Above is a painting Sam did of a little neighbor boy. Above right is some of his contemporary sculpture made into fine porcelain: the Corinthian Collection by Enesco Imports.

Entertainment for the Butcher
family is simple and homemade and almost any occasion
is reason enough for a picnic.
Above: a family picnic takes
place on the porch of the
guest cottage, located on
Center Creek. Top: Katie
bakes bread. Opposite page:
she shares her album of
nature photographs with Sam.
The old rocker was her
Christmas present from Sam
many years ago.

Sam enjoys quiet times with
his son-in-law Steve, and often
they go for a bicycle ride or
into town for a cup of coffee
while Katie spends time with
Jon and Tim playing original
music. Opposite page: the
chapel Sam is building rises
majestically from the hillside.
Inside, the ceilings and walls
will be painted with stories of
the Bible in Precious Moments.

"If any suffer on the way to someone's greatness it's the family. They are the ones that sacrifice and if success should come they too deserve the accolades."

Overleaf: a gallery of Butcher family snapshots. Above, from left: Sam, Hank, Mrs. Butcher, Chuck, Dawn and Ray. Right: Dawn and Ray stand behind Sam (on the left) and Chuck. One of Sam's childhood memories is of his mother making little bib overalls for him and his brothers out of flour sacks.

W hen Samuel John Butcher came unexpectedly into the world on January 1, 1939, party-goers in Jackson, Michigan, were too busy celebrating the passing of the old year to realize that a celebrated artist of the future was making his debut. The night was cold and highway crews were out sanding down the slick city streets so the revelers could get home safely. It was twenty-seven degrees, but warmer weather was predicted and, along with the hope of warmer weather, there was hope for better times in the hearts of the celebrants.

Frank D. Fitzgerald was being inaugurated later that day as governor of the state. The Great Depression was drawing to a close and many business leaders were predicting an upswing in employment and a brighter economic future.

Parties continued throughout the night all over Jackson, a city of 49,000 inhabitants. Among the party-goers that night were Leon Donald Butcher, a hard-drinking mechanic of English-Irish descent with an earthy personality and his young, dark-haired wife, Evelyn Mae Curry, who was of Lebanese and Syrian ancestry. The young couple's merrymaking was cut short by the birth of their third child, Samuel John, the first birth to be recorded in Jackson County that year.

The Early Years

Perhaps it was being born on that day, under those circumstances, that made this child feel different, and isolated from the rest of the family. He didn't like hot rods and motorcycles, and because he couldn't relate to the things his father and brothers were interested in, most of the time he felt ignored or intimidated. "It's strange," recalls Sam's older brother, Ray, "but I can't remember anything at all about Sammy from those early days. I can remember things about every one of the other kids, but somehow Sam was never in the picture; I never even noticed him."

Because he was alone much of the time, Sam created his own joy, spending hours and hours under the table writing stories and illustrating them. One of his earliest childhood memories is of jumping out of bed and hurrying to the dump where he would look for old rolls of wallpaper or unused office pads for drawing paper.

His parents recognized that he was a gifted child at a very early age and began to pay attention to him. "But that eventually caused a wedge between us and I became an oddity all over again," Sam recalls.

"When things would happen, like my parents fighting or a pet dying, it would throw me into a trauma. But it didn't seem to bother the other kids as much as it bothered me and I would wonder 'Don't they feel how I feel?' Because my reaction was so different it only confirmed my belief that I was different. But, really, I had a happy childhood. Because I fantasized. I was a king when I wanted to be a king and I was a prince when I wanted to be a prince. I lived in a world of make-believe and therefore, I loved the world around me. I could draw all the friends and heroes that I wanted," he explains.

By the time Sam was in kindergarten, he knew he was going to be an artist. "I also knew I would have to fight for that privilege, since my father thought all artists were strange people." Throughout his life, Sam was constantly reminded by his father that should he pursue this occupation he was destined to die in poverty.

School opened up a whole new world for him. It was a great adventure, because his teachers recognized his talent and gave him encouragement. While in kindergarten Sam illustrated "Little Black Sambo" and made a little box with a crank that worked like a movie screen. The teacher sent him around to all the classes, even to the eighth grade room, to tell the story and show the pictures. "It was really an amazing thing," he remembers. Teachers continued to encourage the young artist throughout his school years, loaning him beautifully illustrated books of the masters. He was ten when the lure of a better job and more money prompted his father to move the family to northern California. They settled in the small, remote mountainous community of Big Bend, and Sam spent many happy hours in the mountains by himself drawing and painting.

"I could never ask my father for anything," Sam recalls. "I remember one time in particular there was a school play and it cost twenty-five cents. All of the kids wanted to go and asked my father for the money. I just stood there — I could never, ever, ask my father for money." But Sam was determined to go to the play and earned his quarter by delivering papers for a cousin.

The ride from Big Bend to Enterprise High School in Redding was sixty-two miles. The children would leave the house at 5:15 in the morning to catch the bus. It was a very long trip twice each day. But even when his brothers quit school to work full-time in their father's gas station, Sam was determined to complete his education. His brothers, though, were paid for their work while Sam, who worked after school and on weekends, was not compensated. He loved school and felt it was important to grow and learn, but he also felt his parents were punishing him for going to school. His only champion was his sister, Dawn. The hours when they did their chores together, singing "Now Is The Hour" and "Harbour Lights" make up some of her fondest memories of him.

Sam loved music. He played the accordian and the piano, and was popular in high school. "I also realized that one way to make people happy was to draw pictures for them. So, if there were those who ignored me, there were also those who appreciated me, and I used my talents freely."

Sam didn't join in the school's social activities, but he was elected president of the sophomore class and vice-president of the student body. He was on the school yearbook staff and the track team. Sam has never walked when he could run, and the track team seemed a good place to expend his energy.

But nothing took the place of art. He remembers his first glimpse of fine art. It was a Goya and "I didn't know who that was, but I remember the painting."

Teachers played a very important role in shaping his life and philosophy. In the seventh grade, Sam recalls, "Mrs. Finncrfrock reached into my very being. She made me feel that I was a very special person. Her encouragement opened up another world for me."

In high school Sam met two of the most influential people in his life: Arnold Wilhelmi and Rex Moravec. Mr. Wilhelmi was his biology teacher and, while Sam admits that he was not terribly good at the subject, he appreciated his instructor's capacity to understand the deeper things in life. Sam remembers that Mr. Wilhelmi shared with him a wonderful illustrated book of animals, and that "it was the way in which he looked at the book and related it to me that made such an impact on my life." Mr. Moravec was his art teacher and is the person Sam credits with teaching him the skill of putting life into his paintings. "He was a talented man who had the unique ability of bringing out the best in his students. Mr. Moravec had a great sense of humor and could relate to anyone."

In the fall of 1957, when Sam was a senior, Katie Cushman entered Enterprise High School as a junior. She had moved to the area that year with her parents, Frank and Willie Cushman. A pretty young woman with a pleasant disposition and a heartwarming smile, Katie also had a genuine interest in art.

She was surprised to find her art teacher was a young man with a big smile and a willingness to help others. She liked him but thought he was "too old" for her. Later she learned that Sam Butcher was a senior who only assisted Mr. Moravec in the art department.

Although they liked each other, "we really didn't talk very much. But we could relate on all levels, spiritually, academically and aesthetically," says Sam. "Katie was a gifted student as well as being everything else Mr. Moravec thought I needed. He would often bring her attributes to my attention." Because of Mr. Moravec's instruction, Sam was awarded a scholarship to the College of Arts and Crafts in Berkeley, California, one of the finest private art schools in the country.

Sam and Katie never had a date and their relationship didn't

One of Sam's greatest desires as a child was to play the piano but his father insisted on his playing the accordion, which he did during the seventh and eighth grades. He was also the Drum Major in the Redding High School Band.

really blossom until he went away to college. He thought about her a great deal and finally wrote, asking her to go steady.

Katie recalls, "When I received the letter I was overcome with joy and quickly asked my mother if she thought I should." Her answer was "yes" and a few days later Sam's class ring arrived, protruding from the corner of an envelope. "I don't know what kept it from getting lost," Katie says.

While Sam was home that winter for Christmas vacation he got up the courage to ask Katie to marry him. It was New Year's Eve, 1958, and they had spent it babysitting for Dawn and her husband, Jack. While driving Katie home, Sam proposed. "I don't really know why. Perhaps I just thought it was the right thing to do. Her mother liked me," he jokes.

"What do you think you would say if I asked you to marry me?" Sam queried. When Katie's answer was "yes," it threw him into a panic. "I ran the car off the road into a pasture."

Marriage

Sam and Katie were married December 27, 1959, at the Evangelical United Brethren Church in Gridley, California. Frank Cushman sold a cow to pay for his daughter's wedding and Katie looked radiant in antique satin and lace. Their brief honeymoon was spent at a little mountain cottage with a small frozen lake in the back where they went ice skating.

They set up housekeeping in a small apartment near the college and within walking distance of a hospital where Sam worked in the kitchen. Most of what he made went for school expenses and apartment rent, Katie remembers. "We never had much money as Sam never made more than $120 a month. We didn't have a car and we never took a taxi; we walked everywhere. We couldn't afford to go to the movies, so we would walk through the bad parts of town and watch the people. Then, too, we would hold hands and walk around the lake. But, whatever we did, we always had a good time.

"Once in a while, if we were expecting company, we would buy a little package of Oreos, but just once in a while. Our diet was very simple. One night we would have stewed tomatoes and fried potatoes, and the next night we would have stewed potatoes and fried tomatoes. Once in a great while we would have fish," Katie explains.

Later Sam worked in a wallpaper store, and Katie remembers: "He wasn't a very good salesman, but he loved to do the window displays. He would bring home wallpaper samples and we would have them all over the floor of the apartment. Sam would draw the designs and I would cut them out and put them together and then shade them in with paints. We were on our knees the first year we were together. There were always deadlines and we were always busy. But we would get

Samuel John Butcher, Redding High School, Redding, California, Class of 1958

together with friends and share a baked potato, tell ghost stories and do homework."

They were both growing and maturing. Sam was breaking away from his family's lifestyle, and that "caused a lot of battles inside of him," Katie says. "Sam's family didn't have a lot of polish. They were rough and they pinched their women in public. They had tempers and in being like his family, Sam was going against his own nature. So, sometimes temper tantrums would surface."

When they found they were going to be parents they were overjoyed. They had both always loved children.

In December of 1961, Katie moved home to be with her parents "because we couldn't afford a doctor." The night before Jon was born, March 12, 1962, Sam came home to be with her and he never went back to school. He got a job at Mercy Hospital and when Jon was only a few weeks old they moved into a hilltop cottage within walking distance of the hospital. When Katie saved up $350 from the nickels, dimes and pennies she found in Sam's pockets on wash day, they bought a tan, two-door 1952 Chevy. "He was really proud of that car," Katie smiles.

"One particular day Sam had left the car in neutral — and here we lived on top of a hill. He came in the door and started talking about the day's events while the car began rolling down the hill. All of a sudden he noticed that it was moving and he began yelling at the car 'Stop! Stop!' Instead of running around the front of the car he ran behind it, and then he couldn't get the door open, so he started jumping and yelling louder. The car ran right into the landlord's garage and almost demolished it. The landlord was furious and demanded that we find another place to live," she laughs.

Then Sam left his job at Mercy Hospital and the once-promising artist who had illustrated "Little Black Sambo" went to work at Sambo's Restaurant. "It was hard. I had graduated from high school with honors and everyone had high hopes for me. I had won a fine arts scholarship and here I was washing dishes at Sambo's! But if I was going to wash dishes, I would be the best dishwasher ever. I was not going to be humiliated," Sam declares. He worked hard and soon he was promoted to cook. "Now I had to be out in front where everyone could see me. But I have always tried to make everything I do a positive instead of a negative, so I thought, 'If I'm going to make Sambo's pancakes, then I'll make Sambo's pancakes' and I would make eyes and a nose and curly hair on my pancakes and I worked extremely fast, so it didn't slow me down. Everyone loved it except my boss!" he concludes. The customers thought it was wonderful, but the boss knew Sam wouldn't

Kathie Eunice Cushman, Redding High School, Redding, California, Class of 1959

27

Most of Sam and Katie's wedding pictures didn't turn out, so shortly after their marriage, they walked four miles to the bus station carrying their wedding clothes in a brown paper bag and had their photographs taken for twenty-five cents each. Above: the before and after photos.

always be around and wanted to keep his customers happy. So even this artistic venture had to come to an end.

"More than anything else I wanted to continue my education and realize my dream of becoming a professor of fine arts, and teach art education. Still, if I couldn't do that I would make the most of the job I had," says Sam. "But God had other plans for me and it was during that time God began to intervene in my life and things completely changed."

Sam didn't know very much about the Lord. He had gone to church with his sister Dawn when they lived in Michigan. She had only been nine years old, but she would get him up and they would go to the Sycamore Baptist Church and Sunday school by bus. When they visited Grandma Ethel Knudsen, she would talk to them about Jesus. But they didn't visit her often as she lived on a farm near Hanover, Michigan.

For Katie it was different, for she had always had a close relationship with the Lord. As a small child she would only sit on half of her chair so "Jesus could sit beside me." At work or play and when she knelt to pray, Jesus was there.

It was Katie who suggested they attend a little church very near their home. Sam agreed and one Sunday the young couple and their two sons, Jon and Philip, who was born June 10, 1963, attended North Valley Baptist Church. Sam was pathetically shy and remembers: "Everything was so new to me. As soon as the service was over I went home and it wasn't until I got there that I realized I had walked off with a hymnal! I was so embarrassed. I couldn't rest until I returned it the next Sunday. It was then I gave my life to the Lord, and very early in my Christian life the Lord Jesus began leading me into the path of fruitfulness and blessing."

In high school Sam had a great personality and he "kind of conned" his way through school. "He was always doing some kind of artwork for his teachers so they would just give him good grades," Katie remembers. "When we married Sam hardly knew how to read. He would read a paragraph and for every word he couldn't pronounce, didn't understand, or found too hard, he would say 'er something' and he would say 'er something' maybe ten times in one paragraph. So you could tell he didn't know what it meant because he skipped so many words.

"In college, Sam loved art history and wanted to know everything about the arts, and he was good at it. But other subjects like English and math stifled him.

"When Sam became a Christian he didn't have the capacity to memorize things, but the Lord turned all that around and the Word was so alive in him that he began to read the Gospels. They were so interesting and exciting that he would memorize verses and pretty soon the verses became chapters.

After a few months all Sam did was work and study the Bible, and he could tell you where any verse of the Bible could be found. It was almost unbelievable. He had had that potential all the time but it wasn't channeled in the right direction. When the Lord gave him direction and a place to channel that ability, Sam was able to comprehend way beyond his previous capacity," Katie explains. "It was phenomenal to listen to him. He could spend a half hour studying the Bible and talk an hour and a half, making the most beautiful correlations and relationships."

Their pastor knew of the young couple's desire to serve the Lord and shortly after becoming a Christian, Sam was offered a job in the shipping department at the international office of Child Evangelism Fellowship (CEF) in Grand Rapids, Michigan. He was quickly promoted to the art department.

His ability as an artist grew and so did his family. Philip was only a year old when Tammy was born on July 18, 1964. Debbie joined the family on January 24, 1966, and Timmy made his entry into the world on June 14, 1967.

In addition to his growing family obligations, Sam's workload for CEF continued to grow and became impossible for one artist. To supplement his income Sam would clean office buildings and then would go home to complete the work he had taken home from the office. He recalls, "I tried to endure the pressure but it soon became impossible. One day I asked my boss if he would consider hiring some help for me. It was then he informed me they were already considering a replacement who would carry the workload without any problem. Needless to say, I was crushed. I was shocked and I felt betrayed. My heart was filled with bitterness and I spent the next three weeks asking the Lord to give me the grace to be kind to my replacement. At last the day came and my superiors brought the new artist to my room." Following a rather cool introduction from his superior, Sam turned around to see Bill Biel for the first time. "He truly had the kindest eyes I had ever seen. God brought us together and from the beginning we were friends," says Sam.

Remembering that first meeting, Bill says, "Sam was shy at first, but he came across in a very warm way. Soon I felt I had known him all my life."

Sam promptly went to work for a lithographer and Bill tried to adjust to the workload Sam had been carrying but found after only a few weeks that it was impossible. So Bill approached his employer and said he really needed some help. "The work they had demanded of Sam was ridiculous. I have never known an artist who could produce the amount of artwork that Sam can. He is the most prolific artist I have ever

Sam painted Jesus Healing the Blind Man *for his Uncle Sam Butcher.*

Although there was very little money and no television when the Butcher children were small, their lives were rich with homemade fun and entertainment. Kate and the children spent hours putting on plays and making puppets. Above: Kate and Jon.

known," Bill declares.

The employer at CEF realized Sam's worth and called him to ask if he would consider returning to his old job. As Sam wasn't enjoying his new job very much, he quickly agreed.

In 1967, prior to Timmy's birth, Katie had been suffering severe headaches and doctors had discovered she had tumors. Her health continued to worsen and, after almost two years, Sam and Katie decided to move to California to be near her parents, who could help with their children during Katie's illness. Sam accepted a job near Redding as Regional Director for Child Evangelism Fellowship. The job only guaranteed $50 per month, "but the Lord provided us with a beautiful little house and we had a garden. Friends who worked at a produce store would bring us vegetables that would have rotted over the weekend. Another couple had a cow and would bring us milk and I churned butter from the cream," Katie recalls, "and other people would bring us clothing. Sam gave in and we got food stamps, which he had never done before, but he felt the family needed the cheese and orange juice and other things we couldn't afford. So we lived well, we just didn't have any money," she explains. During this time Katie wore a back brace and was in bed much of the time. "You could look at her and tell she wasn't feeling well, but she never complained, and she never let her own pain get in the way of serving others," says Sam's sister Dawn.

"Katie was never one to waste precious time. She used the time she spent undergoing painful treatments to pray for others. Always, she was an inspiration to those with whom she came in contact. Her pain and suffering only provided another vehicle for her to honor the Lord," remembers Sam.

Sam, meanwhile, was working at one of the things he loved best—teaching the Bible. As Regional Director for CEF, his job was to organize Good News Clubs for children. Each week he would conduct teacher training meetings in different areas. The teachers would then teach the children at the Good News Clubs in homes or at churches and hostesses would serve refreshments.

At the teacher training classes, "Sam would teach the lessons and the women would be sitting on the edge of their seats. He is a beautiful teacher of the Word of God," says Dawn, who was one of the teachers.

"Sam loves to teach the Bible and gets deeply involved in research. He can hardly wait to tell you," says Katie, who is also a researcher but writes it all down and gives it to someone else to teach. "I love it and I'm thrilled about all the information, but I'm too embarrassed to get up and tell someone else. Sam doesn't mind if he has something to share for he has a very special gift of teaching," she adds.

Perhaps the greatest influence in Sam's life was his uncle and namesake, Sam Butcher of Redding, California. Sam lovingly remembers his uncle as a "very heavy, happy man with the heart of a vagabond," and during those years of struggle Uncle Sam would ask him to paint "sale" signs for his store and would pay Sam in groceries—"which were always worth more than the signs I painted," Sam recalls. "But that was just my uncle's way of showing that he cared." Sam also remembers that as a child his uncle would bring him clippings about "Draw Me" contests and encourage him to enter. "My uncle was the first to collect my artwork, and the one who took the time to drive mc all the way to the Bay area so that I would be on time to enroll for my first semester in college," Sam says.

After two years in California and the birth of their sixth child, Donny, on June 13, 1969, Sam received a phone call from CEF. Bill had quit and they needed an artist. Would Sam come back to Grand Rapids and take the job?

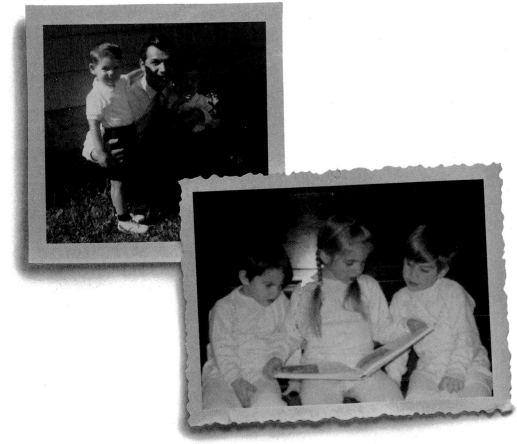

Right: Sam with sons, Jon, left, and Philip, right. Bottom: Debbie reads a story to younger brothers, Donny, left, and Timmy, right.

Sam's most cherished memories are of their little farm home on Orville Street in Grand Rapids, Michigan, where these pictures were taken. Above left: he reads a bedtime story and, left, like all little girls, his daughters enjoy playing with their dolls. A family portrait, below, shows, from left, Tammy, Timmy, Philip, Debbie, Jon and Donny.

"Bill and I were friends before we met and that which we accomplished was God's will. We were destined to a ministry of reaching out and touching hearts through Precious Moments."

Top: Sam with Flo Price, of the nationally televised program The Tree House Club. *Sam was the artist and storyteller on the show, telling Bible stories as he drew them. Above: Sam paints a mural for CEF Mission Emphasis Week.*

*K*atie's health had improved and Sam was anxious to return to working in the field of art, so they packed up their belongings and their six children and returned to Grand Rapids in July 1970. After a very short time Bill found that he was not happy in his new job and asked to return to CEF. So, once again, the two young men were working together.

About one year later Sam became the storyteller for the CEF national television program, *The Tree House Club.* "I would tell a Bible story and then I would illustrate it," Sam explains.

The friendship between Sam and Bill continued to grow and while watching a film together one day they realized the need for visual aids in the Christian teaching field. "It was then we decided to go out on our own as commercial artists. We had no money, just a little bit of poster paint and the talent God gave us," Sam explains. "Because of our close friendship we named our company 'Jonathan and David,' after the beautiful Biblical friendship of David and Prince Jonathan. We fit perfectly together, not only as close friends, but as a successful working team. I was the illustrator and Bill the designer."

Adds Bill, "Sam had a left hand and I had a right hand — our talents overlapped. Sam refused to do the bookkeeping, so I had to do it," he laughs.

It was 1975 and they were doing buttons and Bible flannelgraph backgrounds for Sunday schools and freelance work for other companies, including Mott Media. "They wanted us to attend the Christian Booksellers Convention in Anaheim, California, so they could introduce us as the artist and designer. We didn't really want to go but when they told us we could have a booth of our own I quickly began preparing greeting cards. Bill came up with the name Precious Moments, and that's how it all began," Sam says.

"The cards were the product of a ministry that was rather personal to me. Through the years there were many people who had problems in their lives and needed someone to tell them 'I'm here if you need me,' and I always felt, even as I do now, that I never like to push people. I want to be available, but I don't want to push myself on others. So, my way was to do an individual greeting card. I found people really responded and would say, 'If you would do greeting cards like these so many people would be blessed.'

"The Lord had opened the door for us to begin this greeting card ministry through Mott Media and their arranging for us to attend the 1975 CBA convention in Anaheim," Sam continues. "This was the opportunity for us to develop the ministry of spreading the message of God's love through these little cards. We worked day and night until we had prepared a brochure, buttons and greeting cards to take to the convention."

The Ministry

They also needed a booth for the show and enlisted the help of Dieter Zielke, who attended the same church as Sam and Katie. "They couldn't afford to buy new nails and build the booth so I pulled nails from old lumber and straightened them," Dieter remembers.

Within a short time they were ready for the convention. With Sam sporting a pair of black shoes someone had given to him, they set out for California in an old panel truck.

"We still had to put some finishing touches on the booth and we had to paint it, so when we reached Anaheim we checked into a motel and set to work in the motel parking lot. The manager was furious and would come out periodically, threatening to call the police and have us thrown out. I accidentally sprayed black paint all over the parking lot so I ran to a hardware store and bought a five-gallon pail of 'something' the salesman suggested. To our amazement it ate a huge hole in the parking lot. The manager was really mad by this time and we had to get tar and sand and fill the hole," Sam recalls.

"The next day at breakfast, I was a nervous wreck," he continues. "I was thinking about this big convention and the more I thought of it the more frightened I became. Finally, I told Bill that if last night was any indication of the success we were going to have at this convention then I wanted to get out of here. I went on complaining that people wouldn't like my artwork. I'm always nervous when faced with new situations, while Bill was always a source of strength."

But Bill had heard all of Sam's complaints before and finally he had enough and said, "Look, Sam, before we got here you were the one who was so convinced that the Lord had opened this door for us and now that we're here you don't believe it! Well, I happen to still believe that God brought us here and He will take care of us. So finish your eggs and quit complaining. We still have a lot of work to do!"

"That first day nothing happened, so Bill suggested we start handing out the buttons. Soon people were asking where to get them and swarmed to our booth like bees."

The response was overwhelming. "We had something like $10,000 worth of orders. We were feeling wonderful that night and we celebrated with lots of coke and pizza," Sam laughs.

Now they needed money to produce the cards and fill the orders they had received at the convention, so with the orders in their hands as collateral, they went to the bank. "They laughed us right out of there," declares Sam. "We didn't own our homes and our cars were falling apart," Bill explains.

Sam continues, "Someone suggested we go to the Christian Businessmen's Association. They listened politely, wished us success and said they would pray for us! We had exhausted every possible source and this put us in a position of having to put our trust in the Lord. He was our only hope."

One day in a coffee shop Sam met a man who seemed to be the answer to their prayers. He was very wealthy and offered to loan them the $25,000 they needed to get started in the printing business. "I knew Sam had made up his mind that he did not want to be involved with this man in business, so I told him 'No.' Sam felt all this man had in mind was dollar signs. He didn't have a ministry in mind," says Bill. "After the man left Sam said, 'What do we do now?' and I said, 'Thanks a lot! You were the one who felt he wasn't right for us.' "

But Sam had spent a great deal of time looking to God for answers and studying the Bible. He called Bill one morning and said, "Bill, I really believe we have to stop looking to men for the money we need. I've been studying about Abraham and Lot and the King of Sodom who told Abraham that he would offer him many gifts and Abraham said, 'I will lift up my hands to the most High God lest the King of Sodom think he has made Abraham rich.' "

"I really believe God is telling us that we have to look to Him and not to other people," Bill remembers Sam telling him. "I said, 'okay.' So we started putting the business together like we had all the money and though there were a lot of hardships, at the end of the first year all the bills were paid."

"We needed a building to work in, and the amount of space we needed cost $300 a month. We were devastated because we had very little money between us. But the owner of a building at Three Mile Road was a very kind man and asked, 'Well, how much money do you guys have?' Bill replied, '43 dollars.' He dropped the rent to $40 a month and told us when we got to doing better to let him know and he would raise the rent," Sam recalls. "We were also fortunate to find a printer, Jay Poly, a wonderful man who believed in us and carried us through. And there were many others who helped us along the way, like Dieter who would go around to the malls and pick up boxes for us to ship our cards in because we couldn't afford to buy boxes. And since the post office regulations stipulated merchandise had to be shipped in new boxes, we had another friend at the post office who would slip them through for us."

They never forgot the people who helped them along the way. After Dieter hurt his back and wasn't able to work at his regular job, Sam and Bill showed up with work he could do at home. Dieter has worked for Jonathan and David since then.

Martha Wilbur, who had been an elevator operator when Sam and Bill worked for CEF, was their first employee. She folded Bible backgrounds at first and later counted and sorted cards. "Although Martha had a lot of problems, she dearly

Opposite page, top to bottom: Sam and Bill pose with receptionist Jill Bytwerk at the first Jonathan and David factory, center. The first secretary, Ruth Ringler, is still with the company. This page: Jill, Bill and Sam, below, pose in the new headquarters, bottom.

loved the Lord and trusted Him to provide for her needs. It was the Lord who, years later, directed us to buy a house for Martha." They painted it inside and out with their own hands. Another time, when she was having car problems, Sam and Bill surprised her with a baby blue automobile.

But times were hard during those early years. "We knew nothing about the greeting card business, but we were very creative," laughs Sam.

Trials and Tribulations

*T*he first year we were selling Christmas cards in November. I remember we were in Chicago when we made our first sale (we had to do our own selling as we couldn't afford to hire any salesmen), and this little old lady gave us an order for $500 and it just blew us away! It was a really big order for us. And just as we sold Christmas cards in November, we began selling Bicentennial cards in July! We learned everything the hard way!" recalls Sam.

"Many Fridays Sam would say, 'How about writing me a check, Bill?' and I'd say, 'Well, I could, but you wouldn't be able to cash it!' So we would just pray that when we picked up the mail on Monday morning there would be some letters with checks in them — and there usually were," Bill notes. "The Lord always met our needs, and at very crucial moments. Not always our wants, but He did meet our needs."

One year Sam and Bill painted Christmas scenes on store windows and at garages "to pay our bills and just to survive," says Sam, whose shoe soles were literally tied on with white string. "I remember one lady gave me a pair of shoes," he adds.

"We made all of the Christmas presents for our families. Bill made a rocking horse for his children and Tammy still has the big stuffed doll that I made for her. I bought Kate a rocking chair at the Salvation Army. She still has it — it's the one that sits on the balcony off her studio. We really did sacrifice our families," Sam admits. "But everything in our printing had to be first class and Kate never complained. To me, her life has been so very special. When there was no money it never seemed to matter to her. The only material things she ever wanted were books to teach our children. Those were the only things she ever found any real value in."

Bill remembers Sam and Kate's generous giving nature. "The Lord was just meeting our needs and Sam would say: 'Look over there, Bill! Can't we help them?' He was always concerned with the needs of others, more than with our needs, and I think that character of always being concerned for other people was something the Lord has tremendously blessed. And Kate was the same way. They have always had such a beautiful way of caring for others. I feel that character is why the Lord has

Sam and Bill sell their new Precious Moments products at a convention before they were made into porcelain.

blessed us — because of their being so giving."

Of his wife, Sam says, "There were many years when Kate suffered a great deal, but God used those illnesses to make something beautiful. She was refined as gold is refined by fire so that something great came forth."

"The joy of the Lord is my strength," says Katie. "When I get up in the morning I just bounce out of bed and roll over on my knees. I love starting the day because I am so excited to see what is going to happen. Even when the children were small and we had very little money and no car or television, we played games and made puppets and put on plays. I don't feel my children were deprived of anything."

"The children and I would walk to the grocery store. Each of the children would carry something home and it was a nice outing for all of us. We bought our clothing at the Salvation Army but our children looked really adorable all the time. Maybe I would find a green plaid skirt for Tammy at the Salvation Army and the next day in the mail there would be a matching sweater Mom had found at a rummage sale and a few days later someone would send a pair of matching knee socks. It was never from one source, but from two or three.

"Now to most people this might be a simple thing, but to me it was confirmation that our trusting was what the Lord wanted, so that he could provide for us. It was always used clothing but everything matched and everything fit. Every pair of shoes my Mom would find at a twenty-five-cent sale came at just the right time and would fit just the right child and she wouldn't know that, because she was in California. Mom never knew what we needed and no one else did either, because Sam and I made a pact years ago that we would never tell anyone what we needed. We would tell the Lord and He always knew ahead of time so it was mailed before we realized we needed it."

Even so, there were some hard times that even today they remember with clarity. Once they went to church to hear a missionary speak. "I was so moved by the message," recalls Sam, "that I asked Kate to give me a dollar for the collection. I knew we had three dollars, one dollar for milk and one dollar for gas, and that left one to give to the Lord. I felt I had really done something and it made me feel good. When I handed Kate the plate, she put in the other two dollars. I was really upset and when we got outside I said to her, 'Why did you put those two dollars in the collection? You know that was all the money we had!' and Kate said, 'Giving isn't giving until you give from the bottom of the barrel.'

"I got a ride to work so that was no problem, but a few days later when I came home from work there was no Katie and no

Top: Bill and Sam were often seen clowning around. Above: Martha Wilbur and Babe Moore were Sam and Bill's first two employees. Martha was the elevator operator when Sam and Bill worked for CEF and when they started their own business she became the first employee. Martha's daughter Babe was the second and both are still employed by the Jonathan and David Company.

Jesus Loves Me

Praise the Lord Anyhow

The first four Precious Moments posters were introduced in Atlantic City at Jonathan and David's second CBA convention. They were: Jesus Loves Me, Praise the Lord Anyhow, Prayer Changes Things *and* God Is Love.

children and I began looking for them. It was bitterly cold outside but I found them in a field playing games. I asked Kate what they were doing when it was so cold. She said there was nothing in the house to eat and 'I thought if we came outside and played the children would forget about their hunger.'

"I was so worried. Here I was the father and I didn't know what to do. But there was no sense in staying out in the cold so we went back inside and to our amazement, in the kitchen there was food on the cabinets, and on the table and on the floor. There was a note that said: 'Dear Sam and Katie, we moved to Florida and didn't have a place for this food. Hope you can use it, Pastor Lilie.' " Sam smiles, rcmembering.

During the second CBA convention in Atlantic City, Sam and Bill introduced four posters, *Jesus Loves Me, Praise the Lord Anyhow, Prayer Changes Things* and *God Is Love.* "The public acceptance of the posters was tremendous and although we never received any encouragement from CBA and weren't in the 'in' group, we continued to be blessed by the Lord," says Sam.

Their Precious Moments greeting card ministry continued to grow in acceptance and blessings to those associated with the growing company of Jonathan and David. "Looking back, I was always insecure and Bill was always there to say, 'It'll be okay. They will like your art.' I leaned heavily upon him for advice and design ability and although we were the closest of friends, at times that friendship underwent a great deal of strain," comments Sam.

Many of those times are recalled today with laughter, including the time Sam became so angry he threw a bowl of tomato soup at Bill and it went all over the printing and flannelgraphs they had been working on. This made Bill mad and he hit Sam who fell into the sawhorse that was holding all the flannelgraphs they had been working on for hours!

Another time they became so angry at each other they stopped the car on Michigan Avenue, right on a hill of one of the busiest streets in Grand Rapids, and both of them walked off and left it right there! "But, even worse," Sam recalls, "is the time we were on the freeway in Los Angeles and Bill was to tell me where to turn and when we got right to it, he told me! I didn't have time to turn and I became angry and insulting and Bill became just as angry and insulting and said, 'Let me out!' I stopped the car and said, 'You drive!' and we both got out and stomped off and left the car right there on the road!"

There were funny times, too, like their first trip to the convention in California. "Here I was driving across the desert in this old panel truck and Bill was laying on the floorboard trying to get some sleep. He kept saying, 'It's so hot in here!' I had the air conditioner as high as it would go, but still Bill complained. Finally, after many, many miles, I realized I had the heater on instead of the air conditioner!" laughs Sam.

Sam's blue eyes twinkle as he remembers the time they were scheduled to attend a Sunday School convention in Detroit. "Always our lives revolved around deadlines and this time I was determined we should plan carefully and not have to rush around like mad at the last minute. We worked hard and everything was completed on time. We set out leisurely for the four-hour drive to Detroit.

"When we reached our destination, Bill and I were surprised to find we were the first ones there, so we drove around back and Bill got out and went to the door. I could see him talking to someone. He came back to the car and said very quietly, 'Sam, did you bring the contract?' I said, 'Yes.' 'Did you bring the right number for our booth?' Again I said, 'Yes." Again, very softly, Bill asked, 'Sam, did you bring our Chalk Talk books?' 'Yes.' And then Bill yelled at me, 'Well, what about the date?' We were a week early," Sam laughs.

Through all the struggles, Sam and Bill kept their sense of humor and asked the Lord to guide and direct them in their work of sharing the Gospel through the ministry of the Precious Moments greeting cards. "Basically, they are the results of love, a spiritual love for other people," explains Sam. "And I use children as the subject matter because I feel they are the purest expression of innocence. It was Bill who encouraged me to do the Precious Moments children and the one who originally envisioned the line in porcelain bisque. But we knew that if we were going to produce a procelain product it would take a miracle because we had no expertise in the field and certainly did not have the finances to launch the project. We could only say, 'such as I have I give to Thee, O Lord.' And all we had were some sheets of paper, some paint and the talent God gave us to express his wonderful love."

Early in 1978 they were both in the studio when a man by the name of Eugene Freedman called. He was the president of a company named Enesco Imports Corp. and had seen some of the Precious Moments cards, including *I Will Make You Fishers Of Men.* He was calling from Los Angeles and was on his way to the Orient but wanted to know if they would be interested in making Precious Moments into three-dimensional art. Would they consider having the Precious Moments made into porcelain figurines?

Prayer Changes Things

God is Love

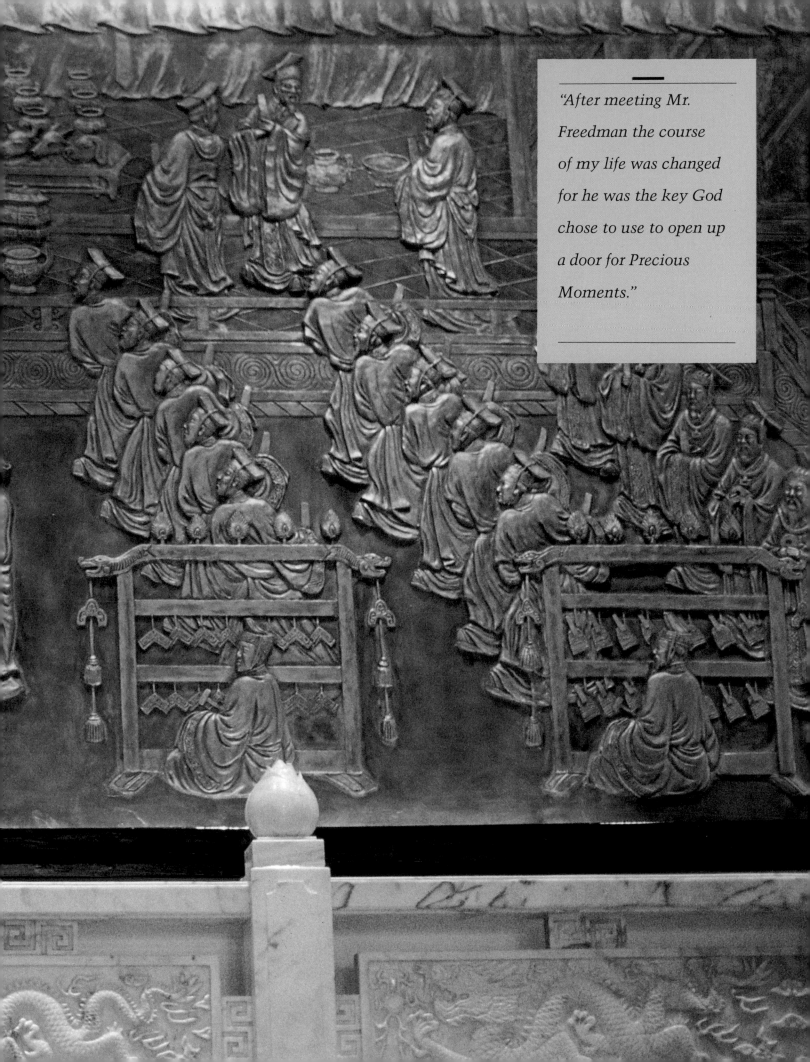

"After meeting Mr. Freedman the course of my life was changed for he was the key God chose to use to open up a door for Precious Moments."

*B*y 1978, Eugene Freedman, president and chief executive officer of Enesco Imports Corp., headquartered in the Chicago suburb of Elk Grove Village, had been involved in the giftware industry for many years. During World War II he served in the South Pacific as a United States Navy ensign and after the war Gene, like many young men returning from the service, wasn't sure just what he wanted to do with his life. He went back to Milwaukee, where he had grown up, and took his first job with a firm that was engaged in dismantling defense production plants and returning them to peacetime use.

He was introduced to the giftware industry early in his career when, in the late 1940's, he took a job as a salesman for a Milwaukee firm that manufactured miniatures. As he traveled the United States, selling miniatures, Gene became familiar with many companies that are still customers of Enesco today. Eventually, in the early 1950's, he started his own company in Milwaukee, which produced injection molded plastics as well as decorative figurines, a business experience that further expanded his familiarity with the giftware field. The company grew to the point where Gene took in a partner and then, in 1958, Gene left the firm he had founded to his partner in order to join another new and exciting venture.

The Enesco Story

The N. Shure Company, a large wholesale merchandising catalog operation and one of the oldest importing companies in the United States, had just been sold. Six of its employees had teamed together to buy the import division and start their own company. Gene became part of this group, and thus Enesco (a natural phonetic progression from the initials of the original company, N. S. Co.) Imports Corp. was formed. Among Gene's responsibilities were the designing and buying of giftware from Europe and the Orient. In the early days of Enesco, he additionally traveled eight states, selling the lines he helped develop.

One fateful day in 1978, Gene Freedman, while enroute to the Orient, made a stopover in Los Angeles for the L.A. Spring Gift Show. What he discovered on that particular visit was something that would change not only his life and the future of Enesco, but also impact the lives of hundreds of thousands of people throughout America.

"A friend brought me some cards and posters that were illustrations of children with soulful tear-drop eyes," Gene recalls. "I knew immediately that these drawings were very, very special." Thanks to his twenty years of experience in the giftware industry, he also realized immediately that he knew the design studio that could capture in clay the warmth and expression of these drawings of special little children.

The studio Gene was thinking of was that of Yasuhei Fujioka of Nagoya, Japan. "I had known Fujioka-San for twenty years," explains Gene. (The addition of "san" to a name in Japanese shows friendship and respect.) "And I was confident that he and his accomplished associate sculptor, Hitomi Kuwashita, could breathe dimensional life into those wonderful drawings of children. I often call Fujioka-San a pussycat because he is so gentle, and gentleness is what Sam's art is all about.

"When I telephoned Sam and Bill," Gene continues, "they were very reluctant. I could sense that the Precious Moments artwork was everything they had in the world. It was like their own children. But I pleaded with them to come to Chicago and let me tell them what I had in mind."

At the time of Gene's call, Sam and Bill had been checking into having the Precious Moments artwork made into porcelain figurines themselves. "So we weren't all that interested in his proposal," recalls Sam. "but we also knew that we didn't have the money or expertise for such a project ourselves.

"Gene seemed very serious and very appreciative of the artwork. Many people had come to us with proposals concerning Precious Moments products, but he seemed to be different. Gene was the one who really seemed to care. So we decided, 'We'll talk to him,' and that's how it all started."

Gene was experienced enough to know that words alone would not convince Sam and Bill of Fujioka-San's ability to recreate the Precious Moments children in porcelain. So he returned from the Orient with a porcelain bisque figurine of a little boy and girl sitting on a tree stump. He recalls with clarity that first meeting with the young Jonathan and David executives. "It was a memorable meeting. I don't ever remember developing an item that received so much attention, was so meaningful to me personally, or was so important to our company's future.

"Sam and Bill were sitting in front of my desk. When I showed them the little porcelain figurine, *Love One Another*, Sam just went right to his knees and cradled the little figurine in his hands as if it were a tiny baby. 'Look, Bill, look,' he whispered. What a thrill it must have been for him to see his artwork transformed into three dimensions.

"It was a tearful moment, so beautiful to behold," Gene recalls quietly. "It was a very special moment in my life too. A real turning point. We talked about many things during that first meeting. I literally poured out my heart to the two of them. This was not a business association, but a very special feeling of concern, love and respect—all the qualities that make Precious Moments art so unusual were part of this very momentous meeting."

Sam and Bill did not commit themselves that day to let the

Precious Moments art be made into figurines, but they did decide to take the little figurine home with them and to let Gene know later of their decision.

Remembering that first piece of porcelain bisque, Sam says, "When I look at anything someone else does with my own artwork, it's sort of like looking at someone else's expression and feeling that they don't read me. But in what Gene showed me I saw possibilities. So I thought, 'Well, if I could work with this man, this sculptor, maybe we could make this artwork into something very special.'"

Gene was back in the Orient when he received word that Sam and Bill loved the figurine but thought it could be even better if they could go to the Orient and Sam could work directly with the sculptor. "Without hesitation I said 'yes.' It was the very best news that I could have heard," says Gene. "Ordinarily we don't do that because of the expense and logistics involved. I knew that even though Fujioka-San spoke very little English and Sam spoke no Japanese, there had to be a meeting of the artists, so I said 'Fine. Make the arrangements.'"

Remembering the first meeting, Sam says, "I think Fujioka-San is one of the most special Oriental people I have ever met. It doesn't matter if he is an artist, or just a person, because he is so sensitive about the work. And for me he's like a breath of fresh air—I don't feel that we are just dealing with business. I am dealing with an artist who can relate to me 'heart to heart.' We are talking about our feelings and our response to a piece of artwork and not about how it is to be produced.

"When I meet Fujioka-San," continues Sam, "it is as though we go off into our own little world. And I always have felt, ever since I first met this man, that we just sort of related, almost as one person. That is very, very unique."

Gene explains, "Fujioka-San is a beautiful, sensitive and perceptive individual who studies Sam's work like a surgeon studies X-rays. When he looks at Sam's art he has a special smile on his face. When he sees a drawing that he doesn't understand, he will ask 'What is the message?' He wants to know so he can capture the extraordinary feeling and inspirational value that Sam puts into his artwork. Fujioka-San and Kuwashita-San, who has been schooled in the Fujioka technique and style for more than twenty-five years, spend countless hours, days and sometimes even weeks sculpting and re-sculpting the clay of these Precious Moments children, who seemingly come to life under their skillful and artistic hands. Today there is a staff of young sculptors under the tutelage of Fujioka-San and Kuwashita-San, dedicated to learning the sculpting skills of these masters so that they, too, may one day be able to capture the sensitivity and brilliance of Sam

Below: Gene and Ruth Freedman posed with Sam and Bill during their first visit to the Jonathan and David Company in Grand Rapids, Michigan. Bottom: Master sculptor Yasuhei Fujioka-San, shown with Sam and Bill, holds a sign indicating that the little figurine, Dawn's Early Light, *is for Sam's sister, Dawn Purington. Opposite page: the first Precious Moments product seen by Gene Freedman was the poster* I Will Make You Fishers of Men.

Butcher's artwork.

"Fujioka-San will not show anyone outside of his studio a figurine until he is completely satisfied with it. He does not compromise and will destroy the figurine and start over as many times as is necessary, just as Sam Butcher does with his paintings. There is a similarity between the two artists in that they are both perfectionists."

Sam and Fujioka-San are very sensitive to each other's feelings. "Sometimes all it takes is a slight gesture and Fujioka-San senses and responds immediately with his emotions. Only God could have created a relationship such as ours," Sam says.

That first trip to the Orient for Sam was his first meeting with the artist who would take his flat artwork and turn it into three-dimensional porcelain. It was also the beginning of an experience that would have a deep personal impact on his life. Sam admits that he has always had a great love for any people of another country. "I have never had feelings of them being different from me. I was very touched by the things I saw in the Orient, especially by the close relationship between parents and children." He was also impressed with the cleanliness of the Oriental people and of their homes and the countryside.

On that first trip Sam and Fujioka-San worked on the Precious Moments sculptures hour after hour. Sam would draw the eyes of the Precious Moments children over and over, and although the artists couldn't communicate verbally, "there was a definite '*kokoro kara kokoro ni*' ('heart-to-heart') communication between the two of them," observes Gene. "You could just sense what was going on between them. There was a tremendous feeling of mutual respect for their different talents."

Now that he had achieved the perfect match of artist and sculptor, the next step for Gene Freedman was to find a factory that could produce the porcelain bisque figurines. Although the Precious Moments figurines were being sculpted in Japan, he realized the cost of production there was rising due to the increase in the standard of living. "This was due to higher paying jobs in the electronic and auto industries, and because of that the labor force was unavailable in the porcelain and ceramic fields," Gene explains. "We decided that if we were going to do Precious Moments figurines and have them affordable they would have to be made somewhere other than Japan."

He turned to a longtime friend, Paul Chang, whom he had met when Paul was going to school in the United States. Paul had worked for Enesco Imports during summer vacations. Later Paul had returned to Taiwan and Gene assisted him in setting up a trading company. It was through Paul that Fujioka-San and Masa Lin struck an agreement to set up a ceramic factory,

Above, Masa Lin, Fujioka-San, Gene and Sam observe the work of a painter in the Pearl Taiwan porcelain factory in Miaoli, Taiwan, opposite page.

Pearl Taiwan, located in Miaoli, Taiwan. It is the home of many skilled ceramists whose heritage can be traced to the very origin of porcelain itself. Since the factory was originally set up to produce earthenware, it was necessary to change Pearl Taiwan's equipment in order to produce the fine porcelain bisque specified for the Precious Moments collection.

According to Gene, Masa Lin is a member of one of the oldest and most respected Taiwanese families. "He is well educated and very attuned to fine art appreciation. As a young man Masa studied classical music and has a very beautiful voice, very rich and full, but his life was without direction. As a rich man, Masa didn't have to have an occupation."

"Masa is very unusual," agrees Sam. "The sweetness of this man does not show on the surface because he comes across like a dictator, but underneath he is a very precious person. And if there is anyone whose personality and bodily animation reminds me of a living Precious Moments person, it is this man."

"I remember being concerned about the meeting between Sam and Masa," says Gene. "Masa is very different from Sam. But Sam instantly established a warm relationship with him and now jokingly calls him 'Masa Care.' (massacare)."

There were twenty-one original Precious Moments figurines painstakingly and endearingly produced at the Pearl Taiwan factory. They were shipped to Chicago, where they were introduced to the giftware trade in the fall of 1978. In addition to *Love One Another*, the figurines in the first presentation were: *Love Lifted Me, Prayer Changes Things, Jesus Loves Me* (both girl and boy figurines), *Jesus Is The Light, Smile God Loves You, Praise The Lord Anyhow, Make a Joyful Noise, He Careth For You, He Leadeth Me, God Loveth A Cheerful Giver, Love Is Kind, God Understands, O, How I Love Jesus, His Burden Is Light, Jesus Is The Answer, We Have Seen His Star, Come Let Us Adore Him, Jesus Is Born,* and *Unto Us A Child Is Born.*

"The response from the retailers was not overwhelming," remembers Gene. "They didn't break down the door! But when the figurines were presented to the public something unheard-of happened. It was as if the public literally took them into their hearts. The little Precious Moments children with their messages of hope and love, of faith and trust, were very well received.

"I knew this Precious Moments line was special. I also understood what Sam and Bill wanted, and they didn't want Precious Moments artwork cheapened in any way. I was the guardian of the artwork Sam had entrusted to me. The figurines were, from the very outset, very well done, but we wanted to do even more for the people who believed in this unique collection. We started enhancing each figurine, paying attention

At the Pearl Taiwan factory, Sam and Gene Freedman discuss the figurine of a little girl praying.

to every detail—the messages, the packaging of the figurines, the booklet tags and all the little amenities—to make Sam's little messengers even more outstanding.

"When we introduced the Precious Moments Collection it was as part of a gift line, not as a collectible. Today many items are introduced as 'collectibles' or as 'limited editions' in a marketing attempt to make them more valuable, but Precious Moments figurines reached collectible status because of the response of the public. Enesco Imports Corp. wasn't, at that time, known as a collectible company," explains Gene. "We attained the status because of the figurines themselves. They, on their own, amazingly made collectibles history and Enesco Imports into a collectibles company."

Enesco Imports Corp. is very sensitive about every little detail of Precious Moments pieces. "We had to bone up on collectibles and bring people into the organization who had expertise in that field. Actually, the success of the little figurines," admits Gene, "is the design—the inspired design through Sam's hands. The message, its sincerity and integrity, and the ability of Sam to express his work through these childlike blessings is what makes the Precious Moments Collection so successful."

On the Move with the Butchers

While Enesco Imports was learning about collectibles, Sam was learning how to deal with success, for with success came growing responsibilities. He was reluctant to change his way of living and his family continued to reside in the same neighborhood. For them, life went on pretty much the same. "We continued to live the way we always had," Katie explains. "It was only at the urging of attorneys and accountants that Sam increased the household allowance."

But for Sam, life began moving at a tremendous rate of speed. He was under constant pressure to attend conventions and make guest appearances. Business meetings took him away from home more and more often. He and Bill flew frequently to Japan to meet with Fujioka-San and approve the sculpting for the figurines, and then flew to the factory in Taiwan to approve the completed product. There were meetings with missionaries and clergymen, and Jonathan and David set up scholarships and foundations for students going into the ministry.

"We were always mindful of our commitment to the Lord and of our responsibility to spread the message of God's love through Precious Moments artwork," says Sam. "It really made us more sober about how we used the money," adds Bill. And as the world's fascination with the little porcelain bisque figurines grew, so did the Jonathan and David greeting card business. It soon became apparent they had outgrown the old

The Precious Moments Collection debuted with these twenty-one porcelain bisque figurines.

trucking garage at Three Mile Road.

"We had our eye on an old warehouse on Monroe Street that was in horrible condition," recalls Sam. "It was an old furniture building and it had stove pipes sticking out the front windows," remembers Bill.

The renovation of the new Jonathan and David headquarters was a laborious task and many times throughout the process tempers flared. Today Sam gives Bill credit for the entire renovation, saying his only contribution was the large mural just inside the entrance of the building.

Bill recalls that he had always wanted to have a gift shop but it seemed the two of them couldn't agree on anything— "until we put up a wall at the entrance and Sam began painting the mural. That kept him busy while I designed the shop."

Sam worked happily on the mural depicting Precious Moments children in various activities. "The basic theme is that the Guardian Angel watches over little children," says Sam.

With the expansion came more responsibility and Sam, always a prolific artist, was busier than ever. He recalls, "I was spending only one or two nights a week at home." Many people were coming to Jonathan and David wanting to license Precious Moments images and there were endless meetings with attorneys and accountants. Sam, never one to sit still, was always uncomfortable.

While Sam busied himself with Precious Moments art, the Butcher family was undergoing major changes. The children were growing up and leaving the nest. Philip married his long-time girlfriend Connie Studebaker and soon the birth of Trish and P.D. (Philip Dale) increased the size of the Butcher family. Later, little Sammy joined the family while Philip was serving with the U.S. Army Medical Corps in Korea. And while his younger brother Philip was busy being a husband and father, Jon joined Jonathan and David as a salesman.

Tammy followed brother Philip down the path of matrimony and she and her husband Carter (Cubby) Bearinger made their contribution to the family with Katie Lynn, Andreah Dawn and Dustin William. The summer of 1983 brought two new additions to the family as Jon wed Patti Gibson of Texas, and Debby married Steven Wiersma of nearby Allendale, Michigan.

Timmy buried himself more and more in his music, composing classical music for both the piano and guitar, and Donny and Heather were happy teenagers just trying to keep up with their older brothers and sisters. Katie's life continued as it always had, centering around her home, her church and her children, but she was saddened by Sam's frequent absences.

Sam, always sensitive to Katie's feelings, knew that she was unhappy with the direction their life was taking, and he knew

Above and opposite page: There are many cozy corners in the Butcher family's home in Carthage.

some changes would have to be made if their marriage were to continue. Because of all the pressures, Sam felt pulled in many different directions. He wished he could just be an artist and get away from the business world. But he also felt a deep loyalty to Bill, and doubted if he could exist on his own.

"Bill is excellent in administration, merchandising and design and I'm simply an artist, content to only paint," says Sam. "But as our company grew it became inevitable that we were pulled in different directions, and as God's ways are not our ways, He brought about a change. Being the weaker of the two, I felt like I would never make it. I was always content to leave the administration, financial problems and other details to Bill while I sat in the corner spilling coffee and painting Precious Moments subjects. How would I ever learn to handle so many things on my own?

"It was an almost overwhelming decision, and Bill and I have a very special relationship, but as an artist, my real desire was to be an artist and not a businessman. So we decided we would part ways. Our friendship, of course, continued." Sam sold his interest in Jonathan and David, Inc., the greeting card company, to Bill in March 1984.

The next step was to move the family to an area where he could just be a husband and father and do his Precious Moments artwork. It was in February 1984 and Sam decided to make some inquiries on his way home from a gift show in California.

During this time, Katie was not sitting idly in Grand Rapids waiting for her husband to decide where the Butcher family would relocate. "I had hung a big four-by-four map on the bathroom wall. And each night Sam would phone and tell me where he was and I would mark his route on the map. Then I would kneel on the floor in front of the map and ask God to guide and direct Sam in looking for our new home."

One night Sam found himself in Joplin, Missouri, in the southwestern part of the state. He spent the night in a Ramada Inn and woke up thinking, "Lord, this is an unlikely place but if this is where I am supposed to be, I'll start looking."

He went into the a real estate office and when they showed him the country home, located on a hill overlooking Center Creek near Carthage it was exactly what he wanted.

After some remodeling, building a studio for Katie and additional bedrooms, renovating the old garage into Sam's studio and building two log cabins for guests, the Butcher family now has its dream home. And, while Sam still must travel more than he likes, here, among the rippling sounds of the river and the melodious, sweet song of the bluebirds, Sam and Katie are content.

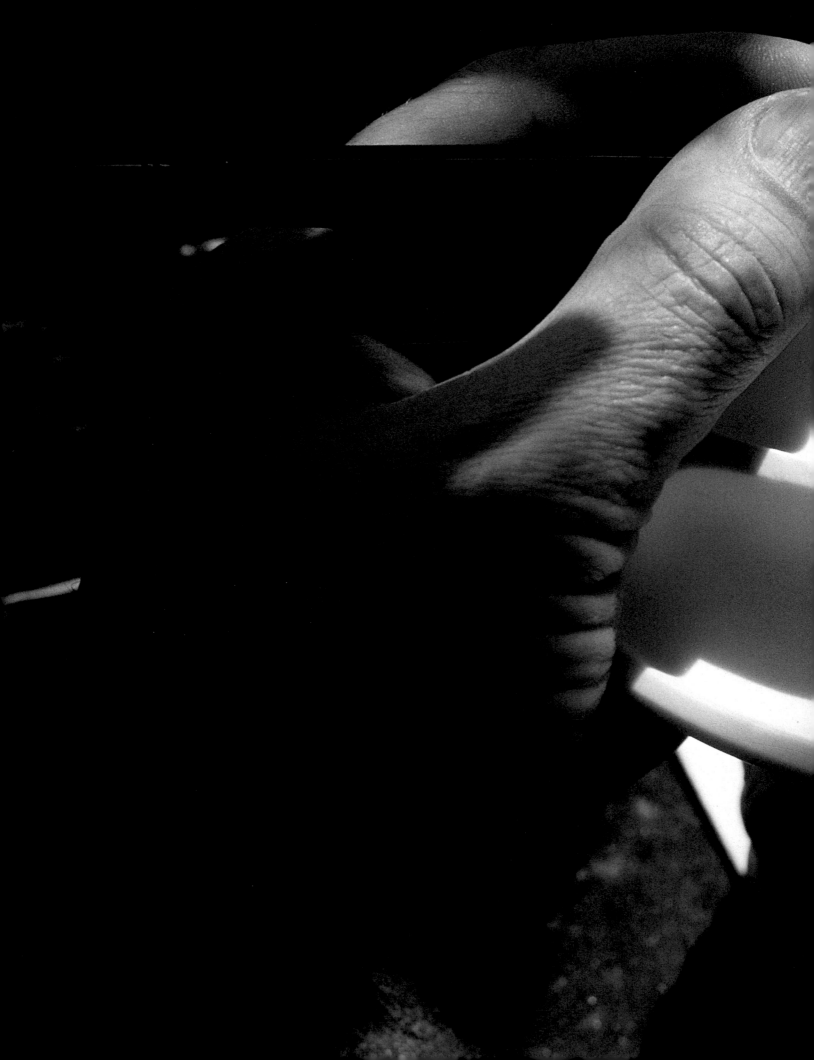

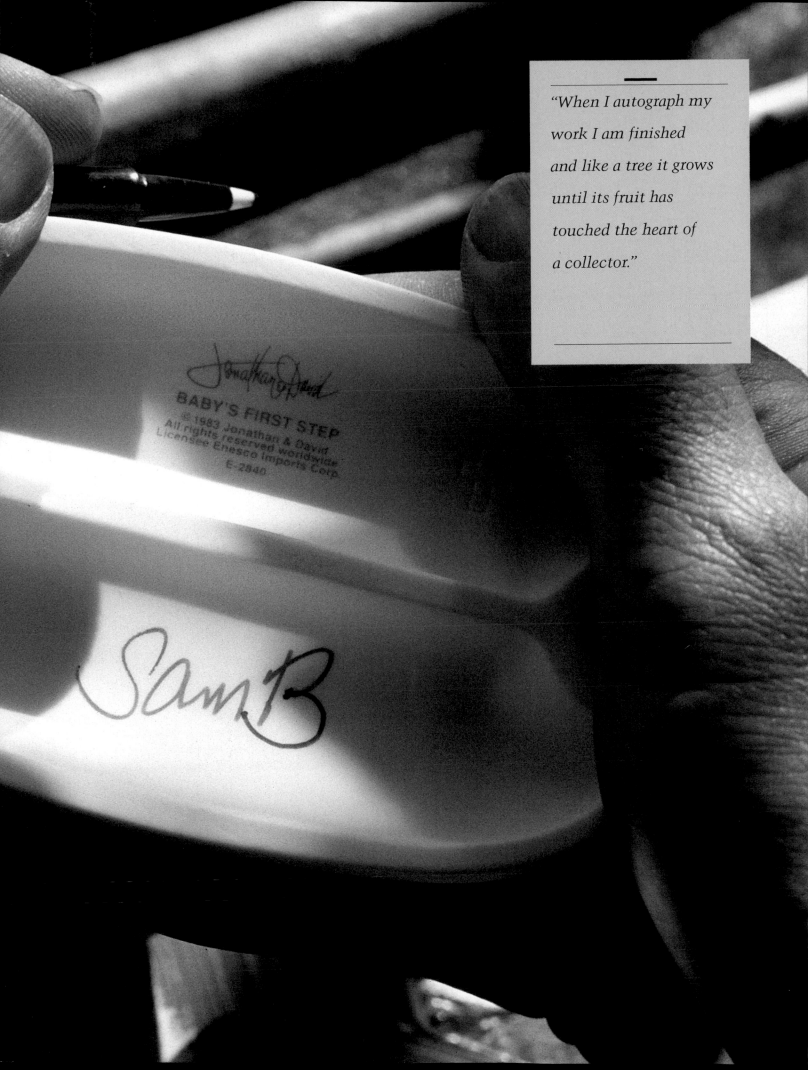

"When I autograph my
work I am finished
and like a tree it grows
until its fruit has
touched the heart of
a collector."

*I*t was in 1979 in Atlantic City that the Precious Moments magic really became apparent, not only to Enesco Imports and the retailers, but also to Sam. Gene Freedman had asked Sam to speak at an invitation-only gathering of their customers, which is not common at shows. But they did not know that Sam had a background of preaching in churches and sharing the Word of God, as well as experience as a storyteller and artist on the national television program *The Tree House Club*. He also writes all the verses for the Precious Moments products.

"But when Sam began to speak, a hush spread over the auditorium. During one forty-five-minute presentation he spoke about the Bible and the crowd was spellbound. It was something very new and different. The audience was amazed," explains someone who was there.

This was Sam's first contact with the people who were involved, on a daily basis, with his "children." It made a great impact on Sam's life, but it also set apart Precious Moments figurines and placed them in a world of their own. Sam's presentation was something never before seen in the giftware market.

Precious Moments art has a message. The artist spoke and touched people. The first collector who touched Sam's heart was Ginnie Meads of Shiller Park, Illinois. Ginnie was dying and felt she had nothing to live for. She started collecting Precious Moments and became an avid collector. She had seen *Love Lifted Me*, and could relate to it, reports her husband, Dale Meads. "The more Ginnie became involved in collecting the figurines, the more she could relate to each one, and each one helped her. There is no denying the messages that Sam is trying to get across through Precious Moments—that *God Is Love* and *Love Goes on Forever*."

With all the fame and adulation, Sam hasn't changed from being the person he always has been, but he readily admits that "Precious Moments has given me a lot of opportunities to do the things I have always wanted to do. But those things still center around the ministry, not just my own entertainment. Precious Moments has been special because of all the people whose lives have not only been touched by them, but have changed as a result," Sam says. "I feel that is the greatest blessing anyone can ever have—to know that our life has touched someone else and given them direction."

As collectors came to want more information about the Precious Moments Collection they also wanted more information about Sam Butcher. As a result, the Enesco Precious Moments Collectors'Club℠ was born.

It was an instant success; in February 1981, in the first issue of the *GoodNewsLetter*,™ it was predicted there would be 5,000

The Collectors

members within the first six months. But by the end of the first year, membership had skyrocketed to an unexpected 69,000 across the nation.

People from every walk of life found they could relate to the little figurines because "Precious Moments pieces reflect situations and emotions we have all experienced," explains one collector. Through the stores that sold the figurines and through the club, collectors shared an instant friendship with each other. They shared information about their collections — the pieces they had and the ones they still needed. They told each other how they displayed them. They talked about their pain and the little messages on each figurine and how those messages of faith and hope, of love and gentleness, kindled a spark that strengthened and grew into very special friendships.

Precious Moments figurines provided courage for those whose loved ones were hurt and dying. Letter after letter arrived at Sam's studio telling how Precious Moments pieces had meant so much to the loved ones they had lost, how the little messages brought them peace.

Brides everywhere began using the figurine *The Lord Bless You and Keep You* on their wedding cakes. Figurines were used in flower arrangements. Collectors named their little boys Jonathan and David and, in many cases, Jonathan David. Some club members were inspired by the award-winning figurine for members only, *Put On a Happy Face*, to dress up as clowns and have fund-raisers. (The proceeds would go to Sam's ministry in the Philippines; see page 240.)

It soon became obvious that collectors were not content with collecting only those figurines that had a special meaning for them, they were adding each and every piece to their collections. When they couldn't find the figurine they needed to complete their collection, they wrote to friends and relatives in other cities, asking them to be on the lookout for specific ones. Soon those who were "just looking" were hooked on the Precious Moments Collection and they were enlisting the aid of *their* friends and families to help them look for Precious Moments figurines. Regional collectors' clubs sprang up. In Holland, Michigan, the club button proclaims: "Holland's Hooked on Precious Moments." Mitzi Taylor of Minneapolis became a collector when three friends joined together and presented her with *God Loveth a Cheerful Giver*. She was hooked. "If you don't want to be a collector, don't ever buy that first piece," warns one man whose wife owns every one of the porcelain figurines.

Carol Crow of West Covina, California, writes, "For me, the little boy angel on a cloud is a witness that my little boy is in heaven. The little angel holding up a little boy on roller skates also reminds me that my little boy who died is helping his twin brother on earth get through the obstacles in life."

"The Precious Moments figurines I bought for my mother who was dying of cancer helped me express to her how much I loved her and let her know that *God Is Love*," writes Doris Willcut of Batavia, Illinois. Caren French of West Paterson, New Jersey, wrote to Sam thanking him for the little figurines. "They touched my heart and turned my path to the Lord. I hope that as I continue my walk with the Lord that His light will shine through me as His light shines through you, so gentle and inviting are His ways."

A thread of courage shows through in the letters from collectors who are suffering with illnesses. One is Kathy Wood who has a rare form of eye cancer. She is working very hard to leave each of her children a Precious Moments collection. "I won't be around to teach them all the things that I would like to, so the messages of Precious Moments figurines will be their legacy from me: *God Is Love, Love One Another, God Understands*." Sam was also touched by Red Ezelle of Macon, Georgia: "A precious boy who was raised in an orphanage. Red collects every piece of Precious Moments collectibles and says that now he has a family, and it's Precious Moments."

The phenomenon grew so rapidly that it was amazing to everyone — most of all to Sam. Collectors began to notice differences in the figurines: errors, misspelled words, and that the little boy with the turtle, *Love Is Kind*, is the only figurine without a hole in the base. Many collectors look at Precious Moments collectibles as an investment and hold membership in the club simply so they can take advantage of the "members-only" pieces that Enesco releases each year. Knowing these figurines will never be released again, these collectors sign up their children, husbands, grandparents and, in some cases, their pets, as members.

The most valuable figurines on the secondary market are those made from 1979 to 1981 that are unmarked or have triangles molded into the figurine's base. The "Girl With Puppies," as it is called by collectors, made in 1978, has sold for as high as $1,000, but the average price for this figurine, whose true name is *God Loveth a Cheerful Giver*, ranges from $500 to $600.

One collector from California reports she made $1,000 in one hour at the Swap and Sell at the Enesco Precious Moments Round Up in Kansas City in 1985 and "I only sold two figurines!" Collecting Precious Moments figurines paid off handsomely for one man who reportedly sold a complete set for $18,000, and used it as a down payment on a house.

There are many such stories to be heard at Precious Moments events, and there is no event as successful as the annual

Top: Sam and his assistant, Dallie Miessner, take part in a Precious Moments Regional Event in Kansas City, Missouri. Above: Sam takes a ride with a young man who came by motorcycle to an event at the Magic Sleigh in Vermont so that Sam could sign his figurines. Opposite page: A Precious Moments wedding was a special event at Bronner's Christmas Decorations Shop in Frankenmuth, Michigan.

International Plate Collectors Convention in South Bend, Indiana. In July 1984, fourteen thousand collectors assembled. Some had come from as far away as Florida and the state of Washington. Many had come to see and hear Sam Butcher.

At the South Bend show in 1985, Sam was not in attendance, but his following still turned out by the thousands. At the Enesco booth, Taiwanese women flown in from the factory demonstrated how the porcelain pieces are individually hand-painted. Larger-than-life Precious Moments "kids," made under the supervision of Fujioka-San in his studio in Japan and flown to the United States for the fifth birthday celebration, stole the hearts of collectors, who patiently waited to have their pictures taken with them.

Knowing that there are thousands of collectors who cannot travel great distances to meet Sam, the Enesco Precious Moments Collectors Club makes arrangements for him to appear at regional events. Many of the same collectors show up at each special occasion. Sometimes they wait in line for as long as three or four hours to speak to Sam, touch his hand, to have him autograph a figurine. When the soft-spoken artist reaches the podium to speak in a quiet, conversational tone, tape recorders throughout the auditorium are turned on to capture his message. From these tapes others are made, and Sam's words reach families and friends around the world.

Collectors send Sam pictures of their children, some of them dressed to represent their favorite figurine. Because some of them see their children as their very own Precious Moments, they want to share them with Sam. Some of the children are healthy and happy, but very often they are handicapped, or have special problems and often terminal illnesses. But whatever the age or problem, every one of them has a special message and a special meaning for Sam. Many leave a lasting impression on his heart.

Unlike most artists, Sam has never sold a painting. "I cannot sell a Precious Moments painting," he explains. "It is not my way. I'll give one away, but I won't sell one. Maybe that is unusual, and it's not because I can't—I just won't." It is nothing for Sam to sit down and do a painting for someone, but he continues to decline all offers to sell.

People who have an original Precious Moments painting know they have something very special, notes one such collector. Sam is often inspired by someone to do a painting and then that painting goes to a particular person. "The Lord hasn't directed me to sell my Precious Moments paintings, but He has shown me many times that I have to do one as a gift," says Sam.

He continues, "One of the most beautiful things about Pre-

Top photos: Sam meets with
collectors; Katie looks on
as Sam signs figurines
at an event in Minnesota.
Left: several of Sam's children
give him a helping hand at the
Precious Moments look-alike
contest in Kansas City.

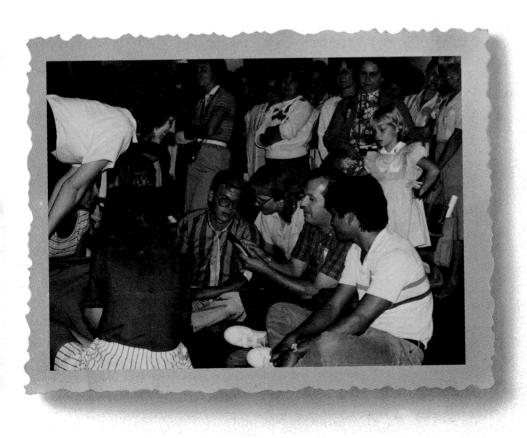

cious Moments art is that there are so many people, from all walks of life, who collect them. That makes it a very different collectible. There are so many people who pick up a Precious Moment figurine and read the verse and immediately it takes their minds off themselves. They think of somebody and say, 'Oh, absolutely—Sally. This is Sally!" So they send it to Sally and she is touched that it was picked as a gift for her. And so Sally starts collecting, and it just sort of grows.

"There is a beautiful verse in the Bible that talks about this: plant a seed and the seed brings forth fruit. Precious Moments art is just the seed in the ground that has been planted and the fruit that it bears is the lives it touches. You know Jesus said, 'You have not chosen me, but I have chosen you and ordained you that you bring forth much fruit.' That's what I see in Precious Moments."

Sam remembers vividly the very first time he did a Precious Moments painting. He made a card of it; it is a little girl with a bird, which is now in porcelain, *His Eye Is On the Sparrow*. But for this particular card Sam called it *God Understands Who Holds the Future In His Hands*.

Sam had made the card for a man he had just met. The man's son had committed suicide after returning from the war. The parents were Christians, but they just didn't know how to handle this tragic loss. And of course many people sent cards and tried to console them, but nothing seemed to help. Sam felt compelled to do the drawing. "I made an original card and sent it to them like all the others who had sent their sympathy."

After receiving the card the man told Sam that the card had touched him and his wife in such a way that they were able to handle the problem. "I don't know how we could have handled it, but that card just gave us the hope of knowing that God had it in His hands from the beginning," he said.

That was when Sam realized the magic and impact that Precious Moments images could have on people's lives. "I don't look at my work as an individual effort," he says, "but as a joint expression that reaches out to others. Without God's help my work would have no meaning. Somehow when one attains success, he soon forgets how he got there. We are not an island unto ourselves. Others have a part in what we are. In the spiritual realm, the Lord is not hindered by our unwillingness. Jesus said that if man will not testify of Him the very stones would cry out. Porcelain is nothing more than stone and Precious Moments share His word on the base of each figurine."

Precious Moments figurines do speak out. They spoke out to a young man who was walking through a department store. His heart was hurting because he and his wife were getting a divorce. As he walked through the store he noticed the

Precious Moments figurines. He stopped and his eye fell on the little boy and girl sitting at the table with a Bible between them, and he read the message: *Prayer Changes Things.*

The young man was very touched, but he didn't buy it. Later he felt compelled to go back to the store and buy the little figurine. He took it home and set it on the kitchen table. When his wife came home she saw it on the table, picked it up, read the message and she began to cry. Then he cried and they embraced. They were able to save their marriage.

Precious Moments images affect people in many different ways. Some see the childlike humor; for others they serve as heartwarming reminders of God's love, and those who cannot verbalize their needs often use Precious Moments art as an instrument of expression, as did the young man who purchased *Prayer Changes Things.*

Sam's children see Precious Moments images as part of their childhood, for it brings back memories of family situations and playing on Grandpa's farm. They admire their father, perhaps most of all because "he always kept working on his art. With all of us to feed it would have been easier for him to have given up and taken a regular job. But he kept pursuing his dream," says Debbie. Although they see their father in a much different way than do collectors, they realize he is a very gentle person with a shy and giving nature. "He is always reaching out to others," reports Heather.

"He's different than most fathers because he's not protective of us. He lets us make our own mistakes but he is always there for us when we need him," smiles Tammy. "Even before he became famous I was proud to have him as a Dad. He has a wonderful sense of humor and can always make you smile. Actually, he is so playful and so much fun that he's like a grown-up little child." Precious Moments paintings are an extension of Sam Butcher's childlike personality, of his reaching out to others and his dedication to using the talent God gave him to bless the lives of others.

Sam talks with collectors at a store event in Houston, Texas.

"Precious Moments come
and then they are gone.
But if that moment is
captured in a figurine it
will remain for many
years to come."

The vision of Sam Butcher—storyteller, artist and writer— has created the Precious Moments Collection. Sam takes ordinary events that occur in everyone's lives and turns them into universal, sensitive and beautiful pieces of art. One friend explains: "Many people think that since Sam has a ministry of spreading the message of God's love, he must be very quiet and pious, but that just isn't Sam. He has a wonderful sense of humor and is always laughing at things that happen around him. He's a genius! His mind is always going a mile a minute in fifty different directions and he is the kindest and most compassionate of men."

Although Sam Butcher is a wealthy man today, "I asked God to give me a very keen remembrance of what it was like to be poor," he says. He remembers the first royalty payment he and Bill received from Enesco. It was $20,000 and "we shared it with a young man going into the ministry. There is such great joy in giving," he explains. "Both Kate and I feel the same way. Our life was never lived just for our family, but for the needs of others."

Those early years of poverty follow him today. Sam never uses an entire tablet or a whole sheet of paper. He folds the paper over, using one side for sketching and leaves the other side untouched, remembering the little boy who searched through the rubbish pile for scraps of paper to draw on.

Sometimes it is a person, but just as often it is a time or event or maybe even a thought, of those long-ago days, that inspires a Precious Moments painting. "Each one is applicable to a situation that confronts us in our everyday life, and each has a message to lift us up," notes Sam. Sometimes, to convey a message, Sam will select a model that relates to an overall theme. "In painting I do not use a physical model, but instead I paint the soul and the spirit of my subject," he says.

Most of the original Precious Moments paintings are completed within one hour. "After drawing the picture completely, I paint the illustration board with a water-based white paint. As it dries, I apply the color. During this process the white paint absorbs the brighter hues, creating a softness when it is finished. Once I begin to paint, I cannot erase, as it would ruin the final piece," Sam explains.

Every porcelain Precious Moments piece created by Enesco through 1986 is shown in this Gallery, including some of the 1987 figurines. The Gallery includes pieces that have been retired or suspended. The Index on page 250 contains a complete listing of all the pieces in the Gallery, with their dates of issue and current status.

The Precious Moments Gallery

Love Is Kind

The Butchers' son Timmy is often the nature boy portrayed in Precious Moments figurines and is the subject of the little boy in *Love Is Kind* — "the little boy with the butterfly on his head and the turtle on his knee," explains Sam. Tim is the intellectual one in the family and the one that most resembles his father in appearance. He also loves to paint and can play almost any instrument, but his real genius is as a composer of classical music. He is now composing "Classical Rock," and often Jon joins him on the guitar. The two young men are planning to make a recording soon. Like his father, Tim likes to spend time alone, and the family gladly agrees to this. "You can walk into the house after working all day and Tim will be playing the same four notes over and over. Six hours later he is still playing the same four notes. That is why Tim lives alone in one of the guest cottages on the Butcher property."

God Loveth a Cheerful Giver

Sam was inspired to make *God Loveth a Cheerful Giver* by his daughter Debbie, "who always collected strays — cats, dogs, rabbits, birds and even people. It wasn't at all uncommon for her to take in everything from animals to troubled teens. While her friends were spending their babysitting money to buy clothes, Debbie's earnings went to the veterinarian. One of my fondest memories of Debbie is of her walking up to me with a box of puppies in her arms and saying, 'Daddy, do you have any friends who need a pet? I have some puppies here that I would be glad to give away for free!' " This figurine is one of the original twenty-one Precious Moments drawings made into figurines in 1978 and one of the first two retired in 1981. More commonly known as "girl with puppies," it is now selling on the secondary market for as much as $1,000.

Praise the Lord Anyhow

Of his second son, Sam says, "Nothing shakes Philip. You can't be with him very long before you just throw up your hands and say, 'Oh, well, *Praise the Lord Anyhow!*' I remember having all the children in church without Katie. Philip was in a particularly restless mood, so I coaxed him into being good by giving him the money for the collection. All went well until the bread was passed and when Philip started to take a piece I said, 'No.' Then I told him 'No' very sternly when he started to take the wine, and I knew something frightful was going to happen. Philip's face looked like a thundercloud. Lower lip protruding and arms folded, he refused to put the money into the collection. Finally after being threatened with dire consequences, Philip retorted loudly enough for the entire congregation to hear, 'I don't know why I should pay when I didn't get any!' "

The Hand That Rocks the Future

Sam says that the inspiration for *The Hand That Rocks the Future* was something that happened when Jon was a baby. "One day after a one-sided shouting match (I was the one doïng the yelling), Kate sat down to feed the baby. She was so upset that tears were streaming down her cheeks. But to my amazement, I noticed that as she put each spoonful of food into his mouth, she would smile. Now that really grabbed me! I couldn't figure it out, so I asked, 'Why are you smiling when you are crying?' She told me that the baby would digest his food better if she smiled and talked in a soothing voice, otherwise he would cry and wouldn't digest his food. That's why *The Hand That Rocks the Future* was designed for Kate."

Top, left to right:
Jesus Loves Me (girl),
Jesus Loves Me (boy).
Above, left to right:
God Is Love,
Jesus Is the Light.
Opposite page:
Make a Joyful Noise.

Top, left to right:
He Leadeth Me, We Have
Seen His Star.
Above, left to right:
He Careth For You,
Jesus Is Born.
Opposite page:
Come Let Us Adore Him.

Top, left to right:
Love Lifted Me,
His Burden Is Light.
Above, left to right:
Jesus Is The Answer, Unto Us
a Child Is Born, O, How
I Love Jesus.
Opposite page:
Prayer Changes Things.

Shortly after becoming a Christian Sam was offered a job at Child Evangelism Fellowship by the International Director Jacob DeBruin. The job was in the shipping department but he told Sam that he could have a job in the art department as soon as there was an opening. "Kate and I realized this was the Lord's will for us," says Sam, "and we sold or gave away everything that we had acquired during our marriage except for the bare necessities. We also realized that it was going to take a lot of faith. After we had sold our car, my father-in-law graciously drove Kate and me and our two small sons to Grand Rapids, Michigan, in his pickup. Most of our friends thought we were going off the deep end, but we knew this was the Lord's will and we were willing to take that step by faith."

I Believe In Miracles

"I designed *I Believe In Miracles* after God miraculously healed my former partner Bill's eyes. The doctor had given him no hope, and, in fact, had prepared him to look forward to a life of total blindness. But through the power of prayer, his eyes were healed and soon after that happened I sat down and painted the little boy gazing at the baby chick. That little porcelain piece is testimony of the power of a living God who can take a totally insignificant life and use it for His glory," says Sam in amazement. "I also look at my own life. Here I was cooking pancakes at Sambo's Restaurant when I became a Christian and dedicated my gift of drawing to the Lord. I am amazed to think that God would use someone like me to spread the healing message of Precious Moments," he adds. This figurine has become the official gift of Child's Wish, a Texas-based organization for children who are terminally ill. The child is given a wish to meet a famous person. The wish is granted and during the meeting the child presents the celebrity with a gift of the little figurine, *I Believe In Miracles*.

Part of Me Wants To Be Good

"In the Philippines there was a very special young man, Albern Cuidad, who was always getting himself into trouble," says Sam. "He just continued to make one mistake after another, but you couldn't help but love him. He would make a mistake and would say, 'Please forgive me. I really meant to be good.' And it reminded me of what St. Paul said: 'The things that I would do, I do not, and the things I would not, those things I do.' That's why the little boy in the figurine *Part of Me Wants To Be Good* is Albern." He is now a college student in the United States.

Below, left to right:
Four Seasons Series. The
Voice of Spring, Summer's
Joy, Autumn's Praise,
Winter's Song.

94

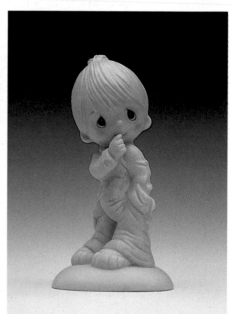

Top, left to right:
Thank You For Coming To
My Ade, You Can't Run Away
From God.
Above, left to right:
May Your Birthday Be a Bless-
ing, Smile, God Loves You.

Top, left to right:
Let Love Reign, Love Lifted
Me, The End Is In Sight.
Above, left to right:
To My Favorite Paw,
Love Cannot Break a True
Friendship, Blessed Are the
Peacemakers.

Top: *Friends Never Drift Apart.* Above: *God Is Love, Dear Valentine (boy), God Is Love, Dear Valentine (girl).* Right: *He's the Healer of Broken Hearts.*

Top, left to right:
Thou Art Mine, Thee I Love,
You Have Touched So
Many Hearts.
Above, left to right:
Love Covers All, Loving Is
Sharing (boy), Loving Is
Sharing (girl).

Top, left to right:
Love Beareth All Things,
Angel of Mercy.
Center, left to right:
Love Rescued Me, Lord, Keep
Me On My Toes.
Bottom, left to right:
Lord, Give Me Patience,
Praise the Lord Anyhow.
Opposite page, left to right:
I'm Following Jesus, It Is
Better To Give Than To
Receive.

Top, left to right:
To a Very Special Sister, Let
Not the Sun Go Down Upon
Your Wrath, Bear Ye One
Another's Burdens.
Above, left to right:
God's Speed, Blessed Are the
Pure In Heart, Jesus Loves Me
(girl, miniature), Jesus Loves
Me (boy, miniature).

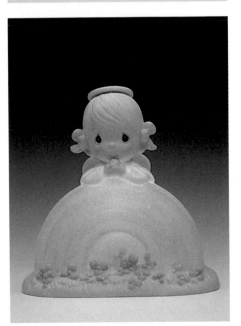

Top: My Guardian Angel.
Above: God Bless You With
Rainbows. Left: He Cleansed
My Soul.

Below, left to right:
It's What's Inside That
Counts, Love Is Sharing,
Nobody's Perfect,
Love Never Fails.

REPORT CARD
Kindness .. A
Mercy .... A
Love ... A
thfullness A

teacher

Top, left: Help Lord, I'm In a Spot. Above, left: Love Is Patient. Above, right: God Understands.

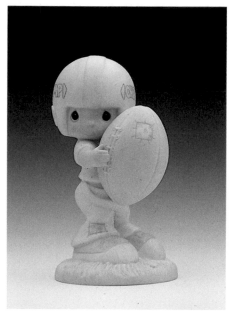

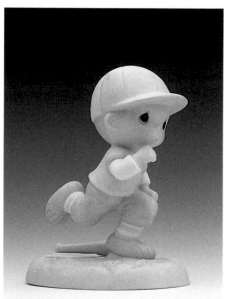

Top, left to right:
The Lord Bless You and Keep You (boy), The Lord Bless You and Keep You (girl), Seek Ye the Lord (girl), Seek Ye the Lord (boy), I'm a Possibility.
Above, left to right:
Serving the Lord (girl), Serving the Lord (boy), Lord, I'm Coming Home.

We Are God's Workmanship

The most frequent model in the Precious Moments line is Katie, who is "gentle, very humble and very kind," says Sam. "She has always inspired the more sensitive and inspirational pieces in the Precious Moments line, like the little girl with the butterfly, *We Are God's Workmanship*. It reminds me of the Psalm: 'I will lift up mine eyes unto the hills...' With all her suffering, Kate has come forth purified and very precious to me." Sam originally did this image as a card of a little girl in a field, called *Autumn's Praise*. "It was a personal card to Katie that said, 'My love for you is always,' " Sam smiles.

To God Be the Glory

Many times Sam's paintings are very personal, and such is the art for the figurine *To God Be the Glory*. "The painting for this figurine was inspired by Psalm 29:2, for it says, 'Give unto the Lord the glory due unto His name. . . .' " Sam explains. "I find this very easy to do in that He has proven Himself to be worthy of the praise because of His greatness in my life. I know it is the Lord who blesses the children I draw and I am not surprised, for it is not my gift, but the Lord's, which He has only loaned to me. He knows my heart, and I am so ashamed when only I am lifted up. *To God Be the Glory* is the testimony of my life."

God Blessed the Day We Found You

Heather is one of Sam and Katie's children who is adopted.
She was born on September 30, 1969, in Grand Rapids,
Michigan, and joined the Butcher family shortly before
her fifth birthday in 1974. Katie had often babysat for
Heather, who lived nearby with foster parents. When the
foster parents decided they could no longer care for the little
girl with the big brown eyes, Sam and Katie decided she
should become a permanent member of their family. "Mama
couldn't let me go because she loved me. So she and Daddy
adopted me," Heather explains. "It was very hard for Heather
to adjust in her first years with the family," Sam recalls. "But
our family accepted her and did our best to share her love.
Now she has grown into a very precious girl of sixteen and the
new adoption figurine, *God Blessed the Day We Found You*,
was created as a token of our special love for her."

Below, left to right:
Miniature Clowns, Let's Keep
In Touch (musical).

Top, left to right:
Waddle I Do Without You,
The Lord Will Carry You
Through.
Above, left to right:
Lord, Help Us Get Our Act
Together, Lord Keep Me On
the Ball.
Opposite page: Miniature
Clown, I Get a Bang Out
of You.

*Above: How Can Two Walk
Together Except They Agree.
Bottom, left to right:
We're In It Together, Scent
From Above.*

Top: Animal Collection.
Center, left to right:
Especially For Ewe, You're
Worth Your Weight In Gold,
To Some Bunny Special.
Bottom: I Get a Kick
Out of You.

Top, left to right:
Sharing Our Joy Together,
God Bless the Bride.
Center, left to right:
Bless You Two, The Lord
Bless You and Keep You.
Bottom, left to right:
God Bless Our Family,
God Bless Our Family.
Opposite page:
Precious Memories.

Above, left to right: Junior Bridesmaid, Bridal Arch, Bless You Two, Flower Girl. Top, right: God Blessed Our Years Together With So Much Love and Happiness. Above, right: The Lord Bless You and Keep You (musical).

*Top: God Blessed Our
Years Together With So Much
Love and Happiness
collection.
Above: Precious Moments
The Wedding Party.*

Top: Forgiving Is Forgetting.
Below, left to right:
God Blessed the Day We
Found You (boy), Rejoicing
With You.

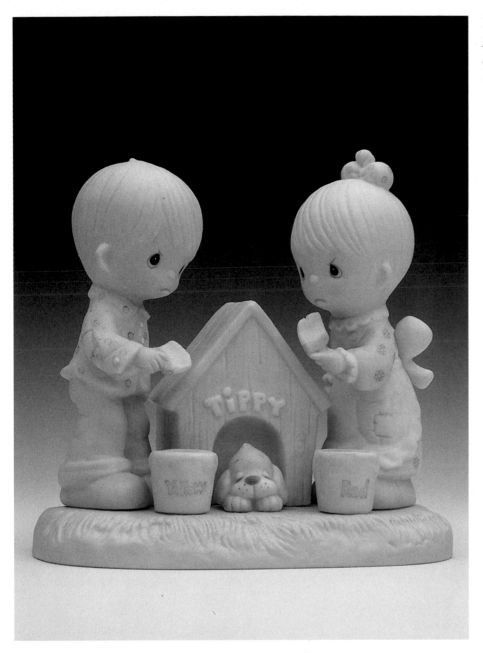

Top: Bless This House.
Below, left to right:
God Bless Our Home, Prayer
Changes Things.

Onward Christian Soldiers

Sam vividly remembers when the idea came to him for *Onward Christian Soldiers.* "So much excitement filled my heart that I could hardly wait to get to the studio to paint him, and after it was completed I just couldn't wait to show Bill. Little did I know that I was introducing my best friend to a little soldier who carried a message that was to pick us up and push us forward during the most heartbreaking, helpless and insurmountable months of our Christian life. As I held this little warrior up to Bill, little did I realize that we would be called upon to wear the same armor as he did. And it was only our Christian faith that supported us and gave us courage as Bill bought my share of the Jonathan and David company and each of us went our separate ways. However, when it comes to those upon whom I reflect as an example of what it means to be a soldier in the midst of crisis, I am reminded of two. One is a man who I believe made the greatest impact upon my life as a Christian and who I believe was the most Christ-like man I have ever known — the late Jacob DeBruin, the International Director of Child Evangelism Fellowship. The other is Kate, who stands like a rock in times of crisis. Through her illness she was tested by fire, and like gold which can be destroyed, her faith, which is more precious than gold, was also tested that it might endure." (First Peter 1:7)

His Eye Is On the Sparrow

Sam remembers vividly the very first time he did a Precious Moments painting. It was made into a card and later into the figurine *His Eye Is On the Sparrow*. But for this particular card Sam called it *God Understands Who Holds the Future in His Hands*. Sam had made the card for a man whom he had just met. The man's son had committed suicide after returning from the war because his mind was "so messed up." The parents were Christians but they just didn't know how to handle this tragic loss. And of course many people would send cards and try to console them but nothing seemed to help. But for some reason, Sam felt compelled to do the drawing. "So, I made an original card for them and just sent it to them like all the other people who had sent cards." After receiving the card the man called Sam and asked if they could talk. The man told Sam that the card had really touched him and his wife in such a way that they were able to handle the problem. "I don't know how we could have handled it, but that card just gave us the hope of knowing that God had it in His hands from the beginning," Sam remembers him saying. Of the figurine, Sam says, "Although I am only a humble artist, God knows my every need. When things happen that I do not understand, I realize that all things work together for good for those who love the Lord, and we can be secure in knowing that as insignificant as the sparrow, the Bible promises that in His goodness and mercy he will see to our every need."

Top, left to right:
Be Not Weary In Well Doing,
Eggs Over Easy, The Spirit Is
Willing, But the Flesh Is Weak.
Above, left to right:
There Is Joy In Serving Jesus,
This Is Your Day To Shine,
We Are All Precious
In His Sight.
Opposite page:
The Joy of the Lord Is My
Strength.

Above: Make Me a Blessing.
Top right: God Is Watching
Over You. Above right: He
Watches Over Us All.

Top, left to right:
To a Very Special Mom,
To a Special Dad.
Above, left to right:
The Purr-Fect Grandma,
The Perfect Grandpa.
Left: Mother Sew Dear.

Top, left to right:
Thanking Him For You, I
Believe In the Old Rugged
Cross.
Center, left to right:
If God Be For Us, Who Can
Be Against Us, Get Into the
Habit of Prayer. Bottom, left
to right:
O Worship the Lord (boy),
O Worship the Lord (girl).

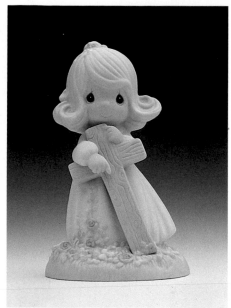
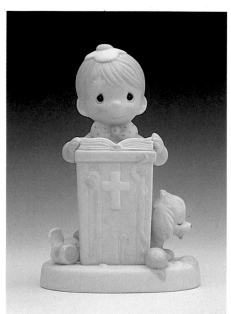

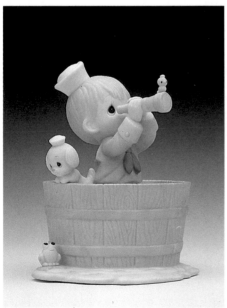

Top, left to right:
But Love Goes On Forever,
Sending My Love, Trust In
the Lord.
Above, left to right:
You Can Fly, My Guardian
Angel (musical, girl),
My Guardian Angel
(musical, boy).
Opposite page, left to right:
Taste and See That the Lord Is
Good, Sending You a Rainbow,
God's Promises Are Sure.

Top, left to right:
Baby's First Step, Baby's
First Trip.
Above, left to right:
Baby's First Haircut, He
Upholdeth Those Who Fall.
Opposite page:
Baby's First Picture.

No Tears Past the Gate

According to Sam: "I painted *No Tears Past the Gate* (Psalm 30:5) to encourage my assistant in the Philippines at the time when his sister was dying. Lea was only eighteen when the Lord chose to call her home. A few weeks after his sister's death I presented the painting to Levi as a reminder to him and to his family that 'weeping may endure for a night, but joy comes in thc morning.' I had hired Levi to work for my company about two years ago and I found him to be one of the most faithful workers I have ever had. In a very short time he was promoted to manager, then to vice president and later to president of the company," says Sam. "Even during one of the most difficult periods of his life and the trauma of his sister's death, Levi proved himself to be consistent in his central responsibility even though at times he was faced with insurmountable problems in the home."

The Lord Giveth and The Lord Taketh Away

"When I arrived home from the Philippines one day," Sam explains, "I entered the house to find myself in the midst of total chaos. Finally, after all the noise had settled down I surveyed the scene and the only thing I could see that had caused the calamity was Kate standing beside a tipped-over bird cage, in total dismay, looking at a trail of bird feathers on the floor. I quickly realized that the cat had eaten the canary. Although it was a sad experience I immediately saw in my mind the figurine *The Lord Giveth and The Lord Taketh Away.*

I'm Sending You a White Christmas

Sam's mother was the inspiration for *I'm Sending You a White Christmas*. Although she was born in Michigan, her parents moved to Florida when she was very small. Following her father's death, her mother moved the family back to Michigan. At that time Mrs. Butcher was only five years old and had never seen snow. When it snowed that first winter the little girl was fascinated by the fluffy white snow. One day her grandmother found her in the back yard making snowballs and putting them into a box. When questioned, the girl told her grandmother she was packing the snowballs to send to all her relatives in Florida who had never seen snow. "It was a very positive thing," Sam says, "and one of the most cherished stories about my mother."

Top: *A Monarch Is Born.*
Below, left to right:
His Sheep Am I, Christmas Is
a Time To Share.

152

Top: God Sent His Son.
Below, left to right:
I'll Play My Drum For Him,
Crown Him Lord of All.

154

Top: For God So Loved the World. Center, left to right: Isn't He Wonderful (girl), Come Let Us Adore Him, Isn't He Wonderful (boy). Bottom: They Followed the Star.

Opposite page, top: Prepare Ye the Way of the Lord.

Opposite page, bottom, left to right: Jesus Is Coming Soon, His Name Is Jesus, Peace On Earth.

Nativity. Back row, left to right: It's the Birthday of a King, Isn't He Precious, Nativity Wall, It's a Perfect Boy, The First Noel, Isn't He Wonderful, Come Let Us Adore Him (four lambs and five figurines), The Heavenly Light, Wee Three Kings (three figurines), Honk If You Love Jesus, The First Noel, Camel, Rejoice O Earth, Isn't He Wonderful. Front row, left to right: I'll Play My Drum for Him, Joy To the World, Donkey, Goat, Tubby's First Christmas, Cow With Bell.

Top: We Saw a Star (musical).
Center, left to right: Joy To
the World (candle climber,
pair), But Love Goes On
Forever (candle climber, pair).
Bottom, left to right:
Jesus Is Born, Bringing God's
Blessing To You.

Top: Come Let Us Adore Him (four lambs and five figurines).
Above: Miniature Nativity Scene. Back row, left to right: Oh Worship the Lord, Come Let Us Adore Him (two figurines), Miniature Palm Tree and Nativity Houses, Come Let Us Adore Him (three figurines and camel).
Front row, left to right: Come Let Us Adore Him (four animals and four figurines), Oh Worship the Lord, Come Let Us Adore Him (two animals).

Below, left to right:
The Story of God's Love,
May You Have the Sweetest
Christmas, Tell Me a Story,
Silent Night (musical),
God Gave His Best.

Top, left to right:
Peace on Earth, Sharing Our
Season Together.
Above, left to right:
Dropping In For Christmas,
Halo, and Merry Christmas.

Top, left to right:
O Come All Ye Faithful,
Surrounded With Joy,
Bundles of Joy.
Above, left to right:
Blessings From My House To
Yours, Wishing You A Season
Filled With Joy,
Christmastime Is For Sharing.

Top, left to right:
To Thee With Love,
Christmas Joy From Head To
Toe, May Your Christmas
Be Cozy.
Above, left to right:
Love Is Kind, Tell Me the
Story of Jesus, May Your
Christmas Be Warm.

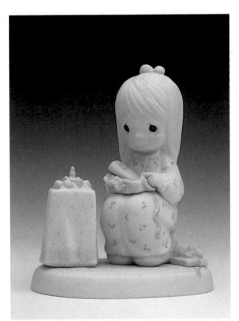

*Left: May Your Christmas
Be Delightful.
Top: Peace On Earth.
Above: May Your Christmas
Be Blessed.*

Above: Our First Christmas Together.
Bottom, left to right: Sharing Our Christmas Together, Our First Christmas Together (musical).

166

Above: Jesus Is the Light That Shines.
Bottom, left to right: Dropping Over For Christmas, God Sends the Gift of His Love.

Left to right:
God Bless America, Brotherly
Love, To My Forever Friend.
Opposite page:
I Picked a Special Mom.

ENESCO'S
PRECIOUS
MOMENTS

HARTER   MEMBER

COLLECTORS'
CLUB

*I*n 1981, just two years after the first Enesco porcelain bisque figurines appeared and ten years after Sam Butcher's artwork first appeared on greeting cards, The Enesco Precious Moments Collectors' Club was born. The hallmark of the club is the figurine of a boy and girl angel on a cloud called *But Love Goes On Forever.* This figurine expresses the spirit of love, joy and reverence that is the essence of Sam's art and, thus, of Precious Moments subjects.

The club was created in response to the desire of collectors to share their common interest to learn more about Sam Butcher and the Precious Moments artwork, as well as to enhance the enjoyment and pleasure collectors derive from Precious Moments collectibles. The initial response to the club was overwhelming; the Enesco staff hoped to have five thousand members in the first six months of 1981 and was stunned to reach that goal within the first six weeks! By the end of 1981 there were nearly seventy thousand. As of May 1986, the club boasts tens of thousands of members.

Club members receive a porcelain bisque "Symbol of Membership" figurine, a national membership card and a subscription to the quarterly *GoodNewsLetter,* as well as a ring binder for back issues of the newsletter, a color brochure and gift registry. One of the most important benefits of being a member is the right to acquire special Members-Only figurines, all of which are displayed on the following pages. Club members also receive prior-to-public notice of figurine retirement and additions to the collection. A special bonus for members is the opportunity to meet with Sam Butcher at regional events that are held several times a year. Membership in The Enesco Precious Moments Collectors' Club is a very special way of sharing the love and caring of Sam Butcher and the Precious Moments Collection.

The Collectors' Club Gallery

Hello, Lord, It's Me Again

Jon, the Butcher's oldest son, inspired *Hello, Lord, It's Me Again* after one of his romantic setbacks. According to his father, "Jon is a handsome boy who had all these girls after him. But the one Jon really loved dropped him and it was a real blow to his ego. He said, 'Dad, I don't know what to do. I have lost the only girl in the world for me.' I answered, 'Sometimes you just have to call on the Lord,' and as I said that I suddenly saw this little guy with a 'Dear Jon' letter on the floor. He's on the phone and there is a tear running down his cheek and he's saying, 'Hello, Lord, It's Me Again.' " Jon did find his girl, and when he married Patti, Sam was inspired to do the figurine *The Wedding Party*.

"God doesn't care if we're wearing fancy new clothes or just had our hair done," says Sam. "It's what's inside that matters. Just as you can't tell a book by its cover, you can't see a person's inner strength from the outside." However, the world too often judges by outer appearances. Sam recalls Bill persuading him to meet him at a men's clothing store, one day soon after the Precious Moments figurines became so popular. When Sam arrived, with white string tied around his shoe to keep the sole from flapping, Bill, dressed very nicely, was already there being given courteous service. The clerks were quite insulting to Sam, but finally one asked if he could help him. Sam went through the store, spending more than $1,000 and, after paying his bill with cash, handed the clerk his business card, pointed a finger at him and said, "And you, young man, don't you ever judge a book by its cover!"

Put On a Happy Face

Sam says that laughter and happiness are contagious. He hopes the figurine *Put On a Happy Face* (which received the 1983 Figurine of the Year award from the National Association of Limited Edition Dealers) will help collectors to always show their sunny side. As he says, "Taking off one's mask to present a happy face isn't always easy. But it's worth it when you see the effect you can have on everyone around you. It shows that you're not just thinking of yourself, but of others." The little clown figurine instantly won the hearts of collectors and soon many of them were dressing up as clowns and entering look-alike contests. One club dressed up in clown costumes and held a benefit for charity.

Dawn's Early Light

This figurine is a tribute to Sam's older sister, Dawn, and represents sentimental memories from his youth of his sister tenderly guarding over him in troubled times. "My sister was a candle in the darkness of my childhood. Even in the most unstable times she had a way of holding things together," Sam recalls. "I remember how, often, after an unsettling night, I would rise early in the morning and run to her room to see if she was there. Her presence was a promise of protection."

Dawn and her family live is Missoula, Montana, and she is, naturally, a Precious Moments collector. She remembers her brother as a "jolly little boy. He loved to draw and from the time I can remember Sam had a pencil in his hands, drawing. He always had a really cute smile on his face — the same smile he has today." Dawn admits she has a hard time realizing the extent of her brother's fame. "I know he is a great artist and well known, but I can never get past the fact that he is my brother."

God's Ray of Mercy

This figurine is a tribute to Sam's brother, Ray Butcher of Redding, California. "The angel depicts the love, caring and kindness that Ray always has for others," explains Sam. "The figurine was inspired by his warm and sensitive spirit. As a child I lived in a world of my own and never really got to know my oldest brother until a crisis drew our family together a few years ago. It was during that time that I discovered this person and his capacity to show gentleness and love in the midst of the most trying circumstances. So many times since then I've seen *God's Ray of Mercy* in the way he handles things." Of his younger brother, Ray says, "In recalling my childhood, I can remember things about everyone in the family, but I hardly remember Sam. It was not because of lack of love, but everyone was busy with their own lives and Sam was always very quiet. No one in the family really understood Sammy, and everything he has accomplished he has accomplished on his own. I know he is a marvelous man and we are very close."

Trust in the Lord to the Finish

Sam's youngest brother, Hank, who now resides in southern California with his family, inspired this figurine. "I began the painting for this figurine on my flight from the U.S. to the Philippines and finished it in my hotel room in Tokyo. Just the day before I left for the Philippines, I had talked to Hank about his lifetime love of driving race cars," Sam recalls. "At the age of ten, he had begun driving the quarter midgets, and as time went on, he became widely known as a driver. Hank's talent took him all across the nation and overseas; he was a champion and the winner's flag was a familiar sight to him. Eventually, however, the roar of the crowds was gone, and the fans had vanished. When we talked, Hank told me about the loneliness he felt and how fleeting his success seemed to be. I realized that those who trust in the Lord have the assurance that Jesus is the same and we can trust Him to the finish. Knowing that all things work together for good for those who love God, we can often find beauty in ashes."

The Lord Is My Shepherd

Sam says, "My second daughter, Debbie, has a personality that most parallels her Mom's. As a result she has inspired some of the more recent inspirational figurines such as *The Lord Is My Shepherd*. Her warm, sensitive spirit has always been a great contribution to the Precious Moments line. In doing this figurine, I was inspired by the trusting way in which she handled a very difficult problem in her life. It is a symbol of God's promise that, He, as the Good Shepherd, is always there to meet our every need."

I Love To Tell the Story

"This figurine was inspired by the old Christian song and dedicated to Pastor Royal Blue of the North Valley Baptist Church in Redding, California, who introduced me to the Lord Jesus," says Sam. "Ever since that time, Pastor Blue has been one of the most important people in my life. He told me to dedicate my talents to the Lord and He would use that talent to spread the Gospel. This may have seemed impossible because I was only a cook in Sambo's Restaurant, but because of God's grace, the Precious Moments collection has touched the hearts of people around the world. While God has given me the opportunity to work in many countries, Pastor Blue remains faithful in his little church, sharing the message of God's love. The figurine portrays his childlike trust and love for the Lord. The child is speaking to a lamb, which symbolizes a pastor feeding God's flock with the bread of life, which is the word of God."

Grandma's Prayer

"My Grandma Ethel will always have a special place in my heart because I still seem to hear her say, "Sammy, Grandma prays for you.' " Sam explains. "Her prayers have followed me through childhood, my school years, marriage and on my trips across the sea. But death has closed her eyes and silenced her faithful prayers. And yet, my grandma's words live on. This figurine is my remembrance of her, and a tribute to her faithfulness in God."

I'm Following Jesus

"I was inspired to create *I'm Following Jesus* after an encounter with a Filipino friend," says Sam. "Carlito, like many in his country, was jobless, but since I had shared the Lord with him, he assured me that he and his wife were trusting in Him to meet their every need. Carlito was formerly a cab driver and since he no longer had a job my heart went out to him. Now he has his own cab which he uses not only to transport customers, but as a special mobile chapel to share his testimony of God's provision and grace in his life. He calls it the 'Katie Cab,' and the sign in the back window reads 'I'm Following Jesus.' "

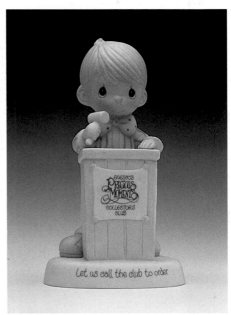

Top, left to right:
Birds of a Feather Collect
Together, Seek and
Ye Shall Find.
Center, left to right:
Join In On the Blessings,
Let Us Call the Club
To Order.
Bottom, left to right:
But Love Goes On Forever
(plaque), But Love Goes On
Forever.

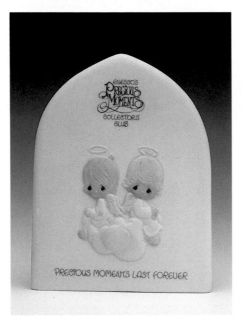

Above, left to right: Birthday Train. Bless the Days of Our Youth, Keep Looking Up, This Day Is Something To Roar About, May Your Birthday Be Gigantic, Heaven Bless Your Special Day, God Bless You On Your Birthday, Happy Birthday Little Lamb, May Your Birthday Be Warm, Our Club Can't Be Beat.

Below, left to right:
Katie Lynne, Debbie.

Precious Moments Porcelain Dolls

The first two Enesco Precious Moments porcelain dolls were inspired by *Debbie*, the Butchers' daughter and *Mikey*, the Biels' son. They were designed by Katie, whose love and sensitivity towards children made her the perfect choice for the project. She is an excellent seamstress and familiar with all the Precious Moments designs, which makes it possible for her to successfully create the soft-bodied dolls, while Sam develops the beautiful heads and hands. For *Debbie*'s clothing, Katie chose a dress of pink print fabric, designed especially for the Precious Moments dolls. Over her dress *Debbie* wears a pinafore of white dotted Swiss, trimmed with white eyelet ruffles and she wears pink bows in her hair. *Mikey* is dressed in little-boy fashion, in tan overalls with sewn-on patches.

These dolls were so delightful that collectors clamored for additional dolls to add to their collections. The next members of the Butcher family to join the ranks of the Precious...

Moments porcelain dolls were *Tammy* and her husband, *Cubby* (Carter Bearinger), who are the bride and groom dolls. Again, these dolls were a collaboration between Sam and Katie, who duplicated the attire of the newlyweds.

The birth of the Bearingers' first child, *Katie Lynne* (named for her grandmother, Katie), who made her debut on September 29, 1982, inspired the Precious Moments doll with her name. This doll was created on January 1, 1983, and, like the girl she represents, has blond hair, big blue eyes and a sparkling personality.

In January, 1984, *Mother Sew Dear* was added to the collection. This became the first doll to be retired, in 1985. Also in 1985, the *Kristy* doll won the distinction of being ...

Top, left to right:
Kristy, P.D., Timmy, Trish,
Mother Sew Dear, Mikey.
Above, left to right:
Bethany, Aaron, Connie,
Candy, Bong Bong.

named Doll of the Year by the National Association of Limited Edition Dealers at the International Plate Collector's Convention in South Bend, Indiana. *Kristy* is named after Bill Biel's daughter. Later that year *Timmy*, the Butchers' third son, joined the ranks of the porcelain dolls, dressed up in a jogging suit, sneakers and all.

Trish and *P.D.*, tiny little babies dressed in pink and blue buntings, won the hearts of collectors everywhere. The two youngsters are the two oldest Butcher grandchildren. Their parents are Philip and Connie Butcher, who reside in Houston, Texas, and whose youngest child, Sammy, is named after his grandfather. *Connie* was also the inspiration for the doll bearing her name, which is limited to 7,500 pieces.

The angels, *Bethany* and *Aaron*, are the first dolls that were not inspired by members of either the Butcher or Biel families. The two children who are the namesakes of the angel dolls were in Katie's Sunday school class in Grand Rapids. When she learned that they were to be the dolls' namesakes, she told them the news, but asked them to keep it a secret, and they did. The angels have wings and halos, but underneath their carefully sewn angel dresses they wear well-tailored undershirts, shorts, tiny stockings and shoes.

The latest to join the Enesco family of Precious Moments porcelain dolls are two delightful clowns, *Candy* and *Bong Bong*. Each of these is limited to an edition of 12,000.

Top, left to right:
1981 Annual Editions, Let the
Heavens Rejoice (ornament),
Let the Heavens Rejoice
(bell); 1983 Annual Editions,
Surround Us With Joy
(ornament), Surround Us
With Joy (bell), Blessed Are
the Pure In Heart (ornament).

Above, left to right:
1982 Annual Editions, I'll
Play My Drum For Him
(ornament), I'll Play My
Drum For Him (bell); 1984
Annual Editions, Blessed Are
the Pure In Heart (ornament),
Wishing You a Merry
Christmas (bell), Wishing
You a Merry Christmas
(figurine), Wishing You a
Merry Christmas (ornament).

Top, left to right:
1985 Annual Editions, Baby's First Christmas (girl, ornament), Baby's First Christmas (girl, figurine), Baby's First Christmas (boy, figurine), Baby's First Christmas (boy, ornament), God Sent His Love (bell), God Sent His Love (figurine), God Sent His Love (ornament), God Sent His Love (thimble).

Above, left to right:
1986 Annual Editions: Wishing You a Cozy Christmas (thimble), Wishing You a Cozy Christmas (figurine), Wishing You a Cozy Christmas (bell), Wishing You a Cozy Christmas (ornament), I'm Sending You a White Christmas (plate), Baby's First Christmas (boy, ornament), Baby's First Christmas (girl, ornament).

*Plates. Top, left to right:
I'll Play My Drum For Him,
Christmastime Is For Sharing,
The Wonder of Christmas,
Tell Me the Story of Jesus.
Center, left to right:
The Purr-Fect Grandma, The
Hand That Rocks the Future,
Loving Thy Neighbor,
Mother Sew Dear.
Bottom, left to right:
Wee Three Kings, Let Heaven
and Nature Sing, Unto Us a
Child Is Born, Come Let Us
Adore Him.*

Plates. Top, left to right: Jesus Loves Me (boy), Jesus Loves Me (girl), Rejoicing With You, The Lord Bless You and Keep You, Our First Christmas Together. Center, left to right: Make a Joyful Noise, Love One Another, Love Is Kind, I Believe in Miracles. Bottom, left to right: The Voice of Spring, Summer's Joy, Autumn's Praise, Winter's Song.

Musicals. Top, left to right: Wishing You a Merry Christmas, Christmas Is a Time To Share, Rejoice O Earth, Let Heaven and Nature Sing.
Center, left to right: Peace On Earth, I'll Play My Drum For Him, Wee Three Kings.
Bottom, left to right: The Hand That Rocks the Future, Let the Whole World Know, Heaven Bless You.

Musicals. Top, left to right:
O Come All Ye Faithful,
Sharing Our Season Together,
God Sent You Just In Time.
Center, left to right:
Silent Knight, Come Let Us
Adore Him, Jesus Is Born,
Crown Him Lord of All.
Bottom, left to right:
The Purr-Fect Grandma,
Unto Us a Child Is Born,
Mother Sew Dear, Love Is
Sharing.

Bells. Top, left to right: Jesus Loves Me (girl), God Understands, The Lord Bless You and Keep You (girl), The Lord Bless You and Keep You (boy), Jesus Loves Me (boy). Center, left to right: We Have Seen His Star, The Purr-Fect Grandma, The Lord Bless You and Keep You, Mother Sew Dear, Prayer Changes Things, Jesus Is Born. Covered Boxes. Back row, left to right: Jesus Loves Me (girl), Jesus Loves Me (boy), The Lord Bless You and Keep You. Front row, left to right: Forever Friends, Forever Friends, Falling For Some Bunny, Our Love Is Heaven Scent.

Ornaments. Left, left to right: The First Noel, We Have Seen His Star, Dropping Over for Christmas.

Ornaments. Top, left to right: Joy To the World, Shepherd of Love, (following four pieces) Come Let Us Adore Him, Wee Three Kings, Unto Us a Child Is Born.
Above, left to right: Have a Heavenly Christmas, Mouse, Our First Christmas Together, O Come All Ye Faithful, Let Heaven and Nature Sing, Tell Me the Story of Jesus, Unicorn.

Ornaments. Top, left to right: Mother Sew Dear, To a Special Dad, The Perfect Grandpa, The Purr-Fect Grandma, Baby's First Christmas, But Love Goes On Forever (boy), But Love Goes On Forever (girl), Baby's First Christmas (boy), Baby's First Christmas (girl).

Above, left to right: Our First Christmas Together, Trust and Obey, Love Rescued Me, Angel of Mercy, It's a Perfect Boy, Lord, Keep Me On My Toes, Serve With a Smile (girl), Serve With a Smile (boy), Rocking Horse.

Ornaments. Top, left to right: Peace On Earth, May God Bless You With a Perfect Holiday Season, Love Is Kind, Baby's First Christmas, The First Noel, Dropping In For Christmas, Camel, Cow, Donkey.

Above, left to right: Joy To the World, To Thee With Love, Love Is Patient (boy), Love Is Patient (girl), Jesus Is the Light That Shines, May Your Christmas Be Delightful, Happiness Is the Lord, May Your Christmas Be Happy, Honk If You Love Jesus.

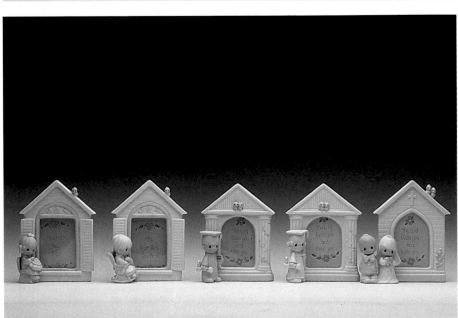

Frames. Top, left to right: Loving You (boy), My Guardian Angel (boy), My Guardian Angel (girl), Loving You (girl).

Center, left to right: God's Precious Gift (girl), Jesus Loves Me (girl), Jesus Loves Me (boy), Blessed Are the Pure In Heart, God's Precious Gift (boy).

Bottom, left to right: Mother Sew Dear, The Purr-Fect Grandma, The Lord Bless You and Keep You (boy), The Lord Bless You and Keep You (girl), The Lord Bless You and Keep You.

Four Seasons Thimbles. Top, left to right: The Voice of Spring, Summer's Joy, Autumn's Praise, Winter's Song. Thimbles. Center, left to right: The Purr-Fect Grandma, The Lord Bless You and Keep You, Love Covers All, Two Clowns, God Is Love, Dear Valentine, Mother Sew Dear. Bottom: Collection Plaque.

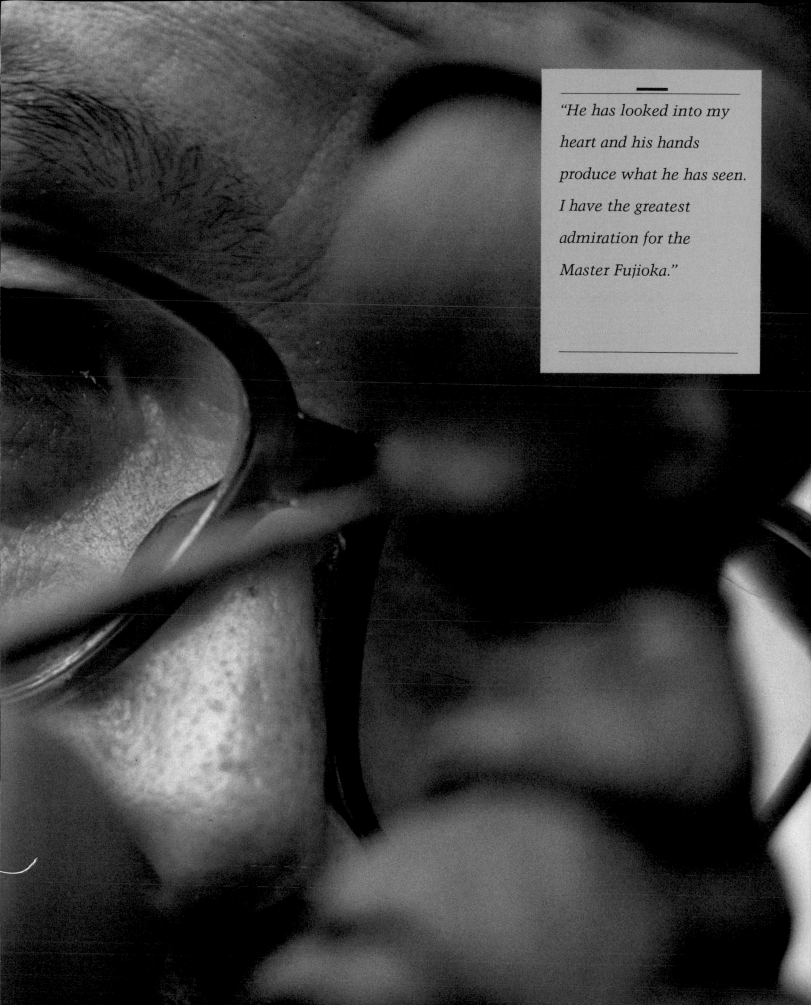

"He has looked into my heart and his hands produce what he has seen. I have the greatest admiration for the Master Fujioka."

*T*he making of a Precious Moment figurine begins in Sam Butcher's studio. Once completed, his artwork is hand-carried to Enesco headquarters in Elk Grove Village, a suburb of Chicago. There, in company president Gene Freedman's office, Sam unveils his art. Sam and Gene discuss the inspiration and what special information Sam wants transmitted to Fujioka-San so that he can capture the spirit of Sam's art, as well as its beauty. The art is photographed and this "portrait" of it goes to Fujuioka-San's design studio.

Fujioka-San sculpts the subject slowly, working in clay until it is transformed, with all its details, into a faithful three-dimensional translation of Sam's painting. Once his clay model has been reviewed and approved, it is carefully cut apart in order that molds can be made. A separate mold is required for each part of a single sculpture, so the original model must sometimes be cut into as many as twelve separate parts.

The molds that are made from the original model are called the "masters." They are used to create six sample figurines. The molds are filled with liquid porcelain, called "slip." The plaster of the molds absorbs the moisture of the slip and, after the slip has set, the excess liquid is poured off, leaving a cavity that results in a hollow part. The casting process used to make the very first sample is repeated on each part of the figurine. Finally, the parts are joined with a mixture of the same slip from which they were cast. The assembled sculpture is now allowed to air dry. It is called "greenware," which means that it has not yet been fired. The master molds are also used to create a set of resin plaster "mother molds." The positive forms are then used to cast production molds of plaster.

How The Figurines Are Made

The sculptures are then baked for more than twenty-four hours at 2300°F in a gas-fired kiln. When they emerge, they are white, translucent and roughly fifteen percent smaller than Fujioka-San's original model. Once cooled, each figurine is decorated by highly skilled artisans, who work from a pastel palette developed to exactly duplicate Sam's. Penpoint fine brushes are used to outline the eyes and accentuate features and details. This decorating process takes as long as that of making the porcelain figurine.

Once the painting is completed and approved, the figurines return to the kiln for a final firing that permanently fuses the color to the porcelain. This firing also makes the colors impervious to light, heat and moisture. Throughout the entire process of creating the figurine, each one is checked by at least twelve inspectors. If any flaw is detected at any stage, the figurine is destroyed. Only those that meet the high standards of rigorous review are carefully wrapped, nestled in their boxes and sent out to win collectors' hearts.

Above, left and right: After the plaster mold is completed, it must be inspected for flaws or imperfections. Often, additional detailing is added at this point. The craftsmanship of the mold-making process is as crucial, and as painstaking, as the process used to make a figurine.

Opposite page: The master mold is opened to reveal the first casting of a new figurine. Overleaf: An artisan's equipment — brushes, sculpting tools, liquid and powdered plaster — enable him to refine the master molds.

Above: Liquid plaster is slowly poured into the mother mold in order to create a production mold. The mother mold is made of an extremely hard resin material and has all of the detail of the original clay sculpture. The resulting plaster production mold will be used no more than thirty times.

Opposite page: An artisan is surrounded by master molds for a variety of Precious Moments figurines.

Opposite page: The production mold is slowly filled with liquid porcelain, which is called "slip."

Above, left to right: The molds are tied together with strong bands of rubber. Each figurine requires numerous pieces of plaster molds, as this shot of the pieces required to create Walking By Faith *illustrates.*

Overleaf: An artist dips her brush into a bowl of slip in order to attach the head to the body of the figurine.

Above, left to right: Parts of a figurine, in the greenware stage, await assembly into the finished commemorative figurine, God Bless Our Years Together. *A craftswoman applies the finishing touches to greenware members of the* God Bless Our Years Together *figurine.*

Opposite page: An artisan smiles proudly as she removes the moldmarks from the assembled figurine, which is still in the greenware stage.

Above: Sam watches closely as a young artisan skillfully applies pigment to his figurine. Opposite page: The mother mold is made of an extremely hard resin material from which the production molds are crafted.

Opposite page: A group of the commemorative figurines, God Bless Our Years Together, *awaits painting. Crafted of pure white, matte porcelain, they are now satin-smooth. Above: The air-dried* Make a Joyful Noise *greenware figurines are ready to enter the kiln for the first firing.*

Above, left to right: The pigments used to paint each subject are the result of specially devised formulas. A technician measures the ingredients needed to exactly duplicate Sam's colors. With care and skill, the artisan — often wielding two or more brushes at a time — paints the delicate features of each figurine.

Opposite page: The Precious Moments Collectors' Club fifth anniversary commemorative figurine, God Bless Our Years Together, *is lovingly painted.*
Overleaf: But Love Goes On Forever *enters the tunnel kiln for the glaze firing. Limited edition collectors' plates are stacked above the figurines.*

"This is my mission field
a place where I can
share God's word by
helping those in need."

*P*eople often ask Sam about the significance of his interest in the Philippines and how it relates to Precious Moments. The Philippines are very significant, Sam explains, as he warmly shares his story. "Several years ago Bill and I were invited to visit the porcelain factory in Taiwan. The experience of seeing Precious Moments artwork transformed into porcelain bisque was greatly rewarding. After our visit we had some free time and we decided to go to the Philippines. About two years prior to that we had met a Filipino missionary who had invited us there.

"Upon arriving in Iloilo City on the Penay Islands, we visited Doane Baptist Bible School, where we learned that thirty-two students were being turned away because they lacked the necessary funds to pay for their tuition. Our hearts went out to them and we were moved to settle their accounts as well as to set up a scholarship fund to finance their needs.

The Philippines

"One year later we decided to open a doll factory there in order to give the students jobs. Because Manila is the business hub of the country, other businessmen could not understand why we would choose a place like Iloilo. After all, it does not have an international port and the students were unskilled.

"We have learned that human logic is not always the premise on which one bases a decision, especially when that decision grows out of a heart of love and concern. Having seen the impossible situation that these students faced, we were compelled to do whatever we could to help them. There were times in the beginning when it would have been easy to give up. The taxi rides on dusty roads to the company each day were anything but inviting. The training of the workers was very difficult — especially when we didn't know much more than they did. But in spite of negative feedback, we were determined to carry on. Through the years we learned together, and to the amazement of our colleagues, the *Jesus Loves Me* dolls produced by the small factory in Iloilo City have been acclaimed as the best-selling doll in the United States during the last six months of 1985.

"Hospitality is the hallmark of the Philippine people, whether they be rich or poor. Many times I was deeply humbled to see them serve their guest the only food they had. To refuse would be an insult, to eat was always painful.

"I believe that God used Precious Moments subjects to open the door of Christian service whereby we could enter in and touch the lives of many. Had it not been for the success of this unassuming line, I could not afford to go to the Philippines. As I look back to see what has been accomplished through the years, I can only sing with a grateful heart *To God Be The Glory* — great things He has done."

One night in his studio in Carthage, Missouri, Sam designed this home, which was later brought to fruition in Iloilo City in the Philippines. Top left: Architect Noney Lim built the house, which will be used as a training center for gifted students. Above left: Reneo, a Filipino student and above right, Reneo with Sam and Katie's adopted son, Joseph.

Top: Capiz shells are gathered from the shores of Capiz and made into beautiful hand-painted wall plates. Bottom: One of the workers in the doll factory.

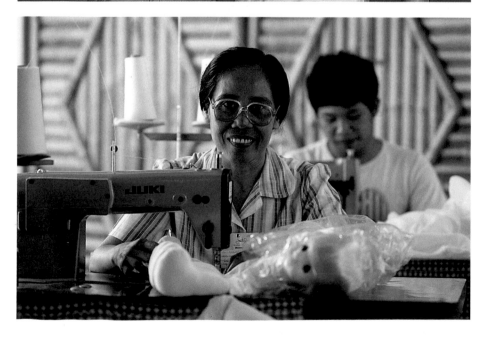

There is an island paradise
Where rugged rocks are hewn
By crashing waves of water
Neath an alabaster moon

A sleepy land of barrios
Where little children play
As flowers open to the sun
Transformed into bouquets

There is a place where trade
winds blow
Beneath the cloudy sky
A momentary masterpiece
That swiftly passes by

Where crimson hills and
fire trees
Consume the vast terrain
My Filipino paradise
Has called me back again

Sam Butcher '86

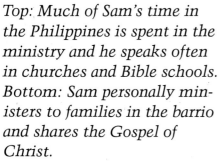

Top: Much of Sam's time in the Philippines is spent in the ministry and he speaks often in churches and Bible schools. Bottom: Sam personally ministers to families in the barrio and shares the Gospel of Christ.

244

Top: This scene is typical of the Philippines. Above left: A child takes part in a festival in Manila. Above right: This young boy weaves palm leaves for mats or baskets in the mountains near Antique.

Sam loves the countryside of the Philippines. Above left: This typical Filipino beauty and Bible student works at the Iloilo City factory. Above right: These children are from a local orphanage near Sam's factory.

"I heard the voice of the Lord saying, 'Whom shall I send and who will go for us?' Then said I, 'Here am I. Send me.' "

Isaiah 6:8

Index

This is an alphabetical list, by category, of every porcelain bisque piece in the Precious Moments Collection made by Enesco Imports Corp. through 1986, including some 1987 pieces. All the pieces listed are shown in the Gallery section of this book. This index lists the name of the piece, the product number, the date of introduction to the public, the year of retirement (if the piece has been retired) and the page on which it is shown. Pieces created for members of the Precious Moments Collectors' Club are indicated by this mark (•) and pieces that have been suspended are indicated by an asterisk (*). (Collectors should note that the suspended status of these pieces is correct as of July 1986 but is subject to change at any time.) In most cases the season (F = Fall, S = Spring) and year of introduction are given; in the case of club pieces only a year is given as they are introduced during an entire year. In the case of 1987 pieces only the year is given, as the season of introduction was not determined at the time of publication.

Figurines	product number	date issued	date retired	pg
Jesus Loves Me (girl)	E-1372G	F 1978		81
Jesus Loves Me (boy)	E-1372B	F 1978		81
Jesus Loves Me (girl)	E-9279	F 1982		102
Jesus Loves Me (boy)	E-9278	F 1982		102
• Join In On the Blessings	E-0104/E-0404	1984		194
Joy To the World	E-5378	S 1984		156
Junior Bridesmaid	E-2845	F 1983		122,124
Keep Looking Up	15970	S 1986		195
Let Love Reign	E-9273	F 1982		97
* Let Not the Sun Go Down Upon Your Wrath	E-5203	F 1980		102
Let the Whole World Know	E-7165	F 1981		137
• Let Us Call the Club To Order	E-0103/E-0303	1983		194
Lord Bless You and Keep You, The (boy)	E-4720	F 1980		107
Lord Bless You and Keep You, The (girl)	E-4721	F 1980		107
Lord Bless You and Keep You, The	E-3114	F 1979		121
Lord Give Me a Song	12386	S 1985		138
* Lord Give Me Patience	E-7159	F 1981		101
Lord, Help Us Get Our Act Together	101850	1987		117
Lord I'm Coming Home	100110	S 1986		107
• Lord Is My Shepherd, The	PM-851	1985		186
Lord, Keep Me On the Ball	12270	F 1986		117
Lord, Keep Me On My Toes	100129	S 1986		101
Love Beareth All Things	E-7158	F 1981		101
* Love Cannot Break a True Friendship	E-4722	F 1980		97
Love Covers All	12009	S 1985		99
* Love Is Kind	E-1379A	F 1978		73
Love Is Kind	E-5377	S 1984		164
* Love Is Patient	E-9251	F 1982		106
* Love Is Sharing	E-7162	F 1981		104
Love Lifted Me	E-1375A	F 1978		97
* Love Lifted Me	E-5201	F 1980		84
Love Never Fails	12300	F 1985		105
Love One Another	E-1376	F 1978		70
Love Rescued Me	102393	F 1986		101
Loving Is Sharing (boy)	E-3110B	F 1979		99
Loving Is Sharing (girl)	E-3110G	F 1979		99
Make A Joyful Noise	E-1374G	F 1978		80
Make Me a Blessing	100102	1987		134
May You Have the Sweetest Christmas	15776	F 1985		160
* May Your Birthday Be a Blessing	E-2826	F 1983		96
May Your Birthday Be Gigantic	15970	S 1986		195
May Your Birthday Be Warm	15938	S 1986		195
* May Your Christmas Be Blessed	E-5376	S 1984		165
* May Your Christmas Be Cozy	E-2345	S 1982		164
May Your Christmas Be Delightful	15482	F 1985		165

Figurines	product number	date issued	date retired	pg
May Your Christmas Be Warm	E-2348	S 1982		114,116
Miniature Animals	102296	F 1986		159
Miniature Clowns	12238	S 1985		114
Mother Sew Dear	E-3106	F 1979		135
Nobody's Perfect	E-9268	F 1982		105
No Tears Past the Gate	101826	1987		144
Nativity Wall	E-5644	S 1981	1986	156
O Come All Ye Faithful	E-2353	S 1982		163
* Oh Worship the Lord (boy)	E-5385	S 1984		159
* Oh Worship the Lord (girl)	E-5386	S 1984		159
O Worship the Lord (girl)	100064	S 1986		136
O Worship the Lord (boy)	102229	S 1986		136
Onward Christian Soldiers	E-0523	S 1983		128
Our Club Can't Be Beat	B0001	S 1986		195
* Our First Christmas Together	E-2377	S 1982		128
O, How I Love Jesus	E-1380B	F 1978	1984	84
Part of Me Wants To Be Good	12149	S 1985		93
* Peace Amid the Storm	E-4723	F 1980		137
* Peace On Earth	E-2804	S 1980		165
* Peace On Earth	E-4725	F 1980		162
* Peace On Earth	E-9287	F 1982		155
* Perfect Grandpa, The	E-7160	F 1981		135
Praise the Lord Anyhow	E-1374B	F 1978	1982	77
Praise the Lord Anyhow	E-9254	F 1982		101
* Prayer Changes Things	E-1375B	F 1978		85
* Prayer Changes Things	E-5214	F 1980		127
Precious Memories	E-2828	F 1983		120
* Prepare Ye the Way of the Lord	E-0508	S 1983		154
Press On	E-9265	F 1982		87
Purr-Fect Grandma, The	E-3109	F 1979		135
• Put On a Happy Face	PM-822	1983		176
Rejoice O Earth	E-5636	S 1981		157
Rejoicing With You	E-4724	F 1980		126
Ringbearer	E-2833	F 1984		125
Scent From Above	100528	1987		118
• Seek and Ye Shall Find	E-0105/E-0005	1985		194
* Seek Ye the Lord (boy)	E-9261	F 1982		107
* Seek Ye the Lord (girl)	E-9262	F 1982		107
Sending My Love	100056	S 1986		140
* Sending You a Rainbow	E-9288	S 1983		141
Serving the Lord (boy)	100293	S 1986		107
Serving the Lord (girl)	100161	S 1986		107
Sharing Our Christmas Together	102490	F 1986		166
Sharing Our Joy Together	E-2834	F 1986		121
* Sharing Our Season Together	E-0501	S 1983		162
Shepherd of Love	102261	F 1986		159

• *club* * *suspended* F *fall* S *spring*

Dolls	product number	date issued	date retired	pg
* Debbie	E-6214G	F 1980		**196**
Katie Lynne	E-0539	S 1983		**196**
Kristy	E-2851	F 1983		**200**
* Mikey	E-6214B	F 1980		**200**
Mother Sew Dear	E-2850	F 1983	1985	**200**
* P.D.	12475	S 1985		**200**
Tammy	E-7267G	F 1981		**199**
Timmy	E-5397	S 1984		**200**
* Trish	12483	S 1983		**200**

Ornaments	product number	date issued	date retired	pg
Angel of Mercy	102407	F 1986		**210**
Baby's First Christmas	E 2362	S 1982		**211**
* Baby's First Christmas	E-2372	S 1982		**210**
* Baby's First Christmas (boy)	E-5631	S 1981		**210**
* Baby's First Christmas (girl)	E-5632	S 1982		**210**
Baby's First Christmas (girl)	15911	F 1985		**203**
Baby's First Christmas (boy)	15903	F 1985		**203**
Baby's First Christmas (boy)	102512	F 1986		**203**
Baby's First Christmas (girl)	102504	F 1986		**203**
Blessed Are the Pure In Heart	E-0518	S 1983		**202**
Blessed Are the Pure In Heart	E-5392	S 1984		**202**
* But Love Goes On Forever (girl)	E-5628	S 1981		**210**
* But Love Goes On Forever (boy)	E-5627	S 1981		**210**
* Camel, Donkey and Cow	E-2386	S 1982		**211**
* Come Let Us Adore Him (four pieces)	E-5633	S 1981		**209**
Dropping In For Christmas	E-2369	S 1982		**209**
Dropping Over For Christmas	E-2376	S 1982	1986	**209**
* First Noel, The	E-2367	S 1982		**211**
First Noel, The	E-2368	S 1982	1984	**209**
God Sent His Love	15768	F 1985		**203**
Happiness Is the Lord	15830	F 1985		**211**
Have a Heavenly Christmas	12416	F 1985		**209**
Honk If You Love Jesus	15857	F 1985		**211**
It's a Perfect Boy	102415	F 1986		**210**
I'll Play My Drum For Him	E-2359	S 1982		**202**
* Jesus Is the Light That Shines	E-0537	S 1983		**167**
Joy To the World	E-5388	S 1984		**209**
Joy To the World	E-2343	S 1982		**211**
Let Heaven and Nature Sing	E-0532	S 1983	1986	**209**
Let the Heavens Rejoice	E-5629	S 1981		**202**
Lord, Keep Me On My Toes	102423	F 1986		**211**
Love Is Kind	E-5391	S 1984		**211**
* Love Is Patient (girl)	E-0536	S 1983		**211**
* Love Is Patient (boy)	E-0535	S 1983		**211**
Love Rescued Me	102385	F 1986		**211**

Ornaments	product number	date issued	date retired	pg
May God Bless You With a Perfect Holiday Season	E-5390	S 1984		**211**
May Your Christmas Be Delightful	15849	F 1985		**211**
May Your Christmas Be Happy	15822	F 1985		**211**
Mother Sew Dear	E-0514	S 1983		**210**
* Mouse With Cheese	E-2381	S 1982		**209**
* O Come All Ye Faithful	E-0531	S 1983		**209**
Our First Christmas Together	E-2385	S 1982		**209**
Our First Christmas Together	102350	F 1986		**210**
* Peace On Earth	E-5389	S 1984		**211**
Perfect Grandpa, The	E-0517	S 1983		**210**
Purr-Fect Grandma, The	E-0516	S 1983		**210**
Rocking Horse	102474	F 1986		**210**
Serve With a Smile (boy)	102431	F 1986		**210**
Serve With a Smile (girl)	102458	F 1986		**210**
Shepherd of Love	102288	F 1986		**209**
Surround Us With Joy	E-0513	S 1983		**202**
Tell Me the Story of Jesus	E-0533	S 1983		**209**
To a Special Dad	E-0515	S 1983		**210**
To Thee With Love	E-0534	S 1983		**210**
Trust and Obey	102377	F 1986		**210**
Unicorn	E-2371	S 1982		**209**
* Unto Us a Child Is Born	E-5630	S 1981		**209**
We Have Seen His Star	E-6120	S 1981	1984	**209**
* Wee Three Kings	E-5634	S 1981		**209**
Wishing You a Cozy Christmas	102326	F 1986		**203**
Wishing You a Merry Christmas	E-5387	S 1984		**202**

Musicals	product number	date issued	date retired	pg
Christmas Is a Time To Share	E-2806	S 1980	1984	**206**
Come Let Us Adore Him	E-2810	S 1980		**207**
* Crown Him Lord of All	E-2807	S 1980		**207**
God Sent You Just In Time	15504	F 1985		**207**
Hand That Rocks the Future, The	E-5204	F 1980		**206**
Heaven Bless You	100285	S 1986		**206**
* I'll Play My Drum For Him	E-2355	S 1982		**206**
* Jesus Is Born	E-2809	S 1980		**207**
Let Heaven and Nature Sing	E-2346	S 1982		**206**
* Let the Whole World Know	E-7186	F 1981		**206**
Let's Keep In Touch	102520	F 1986		**114**
Lord Bless You and Keep You, The	E-7180	F 1981		**122**
Lord, Keep My Life In Tune	12165	S 1985		**139**
Love Is Sharing	E-7185	F 1981	1985	**207**
Mother Sew Dear	E-7182	F 1981		**207**
My Guardian Angel	E-5206	F 1980		**140**
* My Guardian Angel	E-5205	F 1980		**140**

● *club* ✳ *suspended* F *fall* S *spring*

Musicals	product number	date issued	date retired	pg
* O Come All Ye Faithful	E-2352	S 1982		207
Our First Christmas Together	101702	F 1986		166
* Peace On Earth	E-4726	F 1980		206
Purr-Fect Grandma, The	E-7184	F 1981		207
Rejoice O Earth	E-5645	S 1981		206
Sharing Our Season Together	E-0519	S 1983	1986	207
* Silent Knight	E-5642	S 1981		207
Silent Night	15814	F 1985		161
* Unto Us a Child Is Born	E-2808	S 1980		207
We Saw a Star	12408	F 1985		158
* Wee Three Kings	E-0520	S 1983		206
* Wishing You a Merry Christmas	E-5394	S 1984		206

Bells	product number	date issued	date retired	pg
God Sent His Love	15873	F 1985		203
God Understands	E-5211	F 1980	1984	208
I'll Play My Drum For Him	E-2358	S 1982		202
* Jesus Is Born	E-5623	S 1981		208
* Jesus Loves Me (boy)	E-5208	F 1980		208
* Jesus Loves Me (girl)	E-5209	F 1980		208
Let the Heavens Rejoice	E-5622	S 1981		202
* Lord Bless You and Keep You, The (boy)	E-7175	F 1981		208
Lord Bless You and Keep You, The (bride)	E-7179	F 1981		208
* Lord Bless You and Keep You, The (girl)	E-7176	F 1981		208
Mother Sew Dear	E-7181	F 1981		208
* Prayer Changes Things	E-5210	F 1980		208
Purr-Fect Grandma, The	E-7183	F 1981		208
Surround Us With Joy	E-0522	S 1983		202
* We Have Seen His Star	E-5620	S 1981		208
Wishing You a Cozy Christmas	102318	F 1986		203
Wishing You a Merry Christmas	E-5393	S 1984		202

Frames	product number	date issued	date retired	pg
Blessed Are the Pure In Heart	E-0521	S 1983		212
God's Precious Gift (girl)	12041	S 1985		212
God's Precious Gift (boy)	12033	S 1985		212
* Jesus Loves Me (girl)	E-7171	F 1981		212
* Jesus Loves Me (boy)	E-7170	F 1981		212
Lord Bless You and Keep You, The	E-7166	F 1981		212
Lord Bless You and Keep You, The (boy)	E-7177	F 1981		212
Lord Bless You and Keep You, The (girl)	E-7178	F 1981		212
Loving You (boy)	12017	S 1985		212
Loving You (girl)	12025	S 1985		212
* Mother Sew Dear	E-7241	F 1981		212
* My Guardian Angel (girl)	E-7169	F 1981		212
* My Guardian Angel (boy)	E-7168	F 1981		212

Frames	product number	date issued	date retired	pg
Purr-Fect Grandma, The	E-7242	F 1981		212

Boxes	product number	date issued	date retired	pg
* Forever Friends (two boxes)	E-9283	S 1983		208
I'm Falling For Some Bunny and It Happens To Be You	E-9266	F 1982		208
* Jesus Loves Me (boy)	E-9280	F 1982		208
* Jesus Loves Me (girl)	E-9281	F 1982		208
* Lord Bless You and Keep You, The	E-7167	F 1981		208
Our Love Is Heaven-Scent	E-9266	F 1982		208

Thimbles	product number	date issued	date retired	pg
Two Clown Thimbles	100668	F 1986		213
Four Seasons With Figurines On Top (four piece set)	100641	S 1986		213
God Sent His Love	15865	F 1985		213
Love Covers All	12254	S 1985		213
Mother Sew Dear	13293	S 1985		213
Purr-Fect Grandma, The	13307	S 1985		213
Wishing You a Cozy Christmas	102334	S 1985		203

Plaques	product number	date issued	date retired	pg
• But Love Goes On Forever	E-0102/E-0202	1982		194
* Collection Plaque	E-6901	S 1982		213

Night Lights	product number	date issued	date retired	pg
God Bless You With Rainbows	16020	S 1986		103
* My Guardian Angel	E-5207	F 1980		103

Animals	product number	date issued	date retired	pg
Especially For Ewe	E-9282	F 1982		119
To Some Bunny Special	E-9282	F 1982		119
You're Worth Your Weight In Gold	E-9282	F 1982		119

Candle Climbers	product number	date issued	date retired	pg
But Love Goes On Forever	E-6118	S 1981		158
* Joy To the World	E-2344	S 1982		158

Important Note: At the time of publication, Come Let Us Adore Him *(product number E-2800), shown on page 156, had just been resculpted. The new resculpted Nativity set, now product number 104000, is shown on page 159.*

An Explanation Of The Marks

*T*he Precious Moments Collection debuted with twenty-one porcelain bisque sculptures in 1979. (See Index, page 250, for a complete list.) All these share the distinction of being the "premiere" figurines. However, *Love One Another*, which depicts a boy and girl sitting on a tree stump, was actually the very first Precious Moments subject translated from two dimensions into three.

The annual symbol system was introduced in late 1981 in order to indicate to collectors when a figurine was made. The first symbol, seen on figurines made in late 1981, was a triangle. In 1982, an hourglass was used, in 1983 a fish, in 1984 a cross, in 1985 a dove and in 1986 an olive branch. (See below for illustrations of these marks.) These annual production marks change with each calendar year. Some sculptures scheduled for early introduction are created in the latter months of the preceding year, so a figurine introduced as part of a 1984 collection may, for example, bear a 1983 year of production marking. Most of these production marks are incised on the base of a figurine, but an occasional piece has been found marked in ink.

Until 1985, the familiar Jonathan & David signature marked the bases of all the figurines; beginning in that year they are all marked simply Precious Moments, with Samuel J. Butcher's name. Whenever possible the inspirational title of the piece is also on the base of the figurine, or on the back of a plate or on the inside of a bell. Beginning in late 1982, the product number is also printed on the base of the figurine.

1981	1982	1983	1984	1985	1986
▲	⧗	🐟	✝	🕊	🌿